The New Americans
Recent Immigration and American Society

Edited by
Steven J. Gold and Rubén G. Rumbaut

A Series from LFB Scholarly

The Remittance Behavior of Immigrant Households
Micronesians in Hawaii and Guam

Elizabeth M. Grieco

LFB Scholarly Publishing LLC
New York 2003

Copyright © 2003 by LFB Scholarly Publishing LLC

Library of Congress Cataloging-in-Publication Data

Grieco, Elizabeth M.
 The remittance behavior of immigrant households : Micronesians in Hawaii and Guam / Elizabeth M. Grieco.
   p. cm. -- (The New Americans (LFB Scholarly Publishing LLC))
 Includes bibliographical references and index.
 ISBN 1-931202-71-0 (alk. paper)
 1. Emigrant remittances--Micronesia (Federated States)--Sociological aspects. 2. Micronesians--Hawaii. 3. Micronesians--Guam. 4. Immigrants--United States--Social networks--Case studies. 5. United States--Emigration and immigration--Social aspects--Case studies. 6. Micronesia (Federated States)--Emigration and immigration--Social aspects--Case studies. I. Title. II. Series.
 HG3997.6.G74 2003
 339.4--dc21

2003009018

ISBN 1-931202-71-0

Printed on acid-free 250-year-life paper.

Manufactured in the United States of America.

To my father,
who always wanted to write a book
and have it published

Contents

Acknowledgements

My first thanks go to Monica Boyd, John Myles, Carl Schmertmann, and Patricia Martin who provided me with invaluable guidance and assistance while I completed this research. I attribute my skills as a social science researcher to their mentoring, for which I am eternally grateful. I would also like to thank the faculty of the Department of Sociology and the Center for the Study of Population at Florida State University. Their continued support and guidance during my years at FSU ultimately made the completion of this project possible. Mike Levin of the US Census Bureau provided access to the data set used in this research, for which I am indebted. I am grateful for his continued interest and support of this project. I would also like to thank my colleagues at the Migration Policy Institute for their support and encouragement.

CHAPTER 1

Introduction

Since the 1970s, remittances from migrants to Australia, New Zealand, and the United States have played a growing and important role in the economies of Pacific Island countries. Migrant remittances provide capital-poor countries with foreign exchange, ease balance-of-payment problems, encourage industrial development by facilitating the import of capital goods and raw materials, and contribute to employment (Russell 1986; Menjivar et al. 1998). Remittances represent an important component of the total national incomes of many Pacific Island countries, including Tonga, Western Samoa, and the Cook Islands. For example, in the early 1980s, remittances contributed between 35 and 40 percent of the Cook Islands' total income (Connell 1980), while in 1989, remittances represented approximately 60 percent of the Tongan and 35 percent of the Western Samoan gross domestic product (Appleyard and Stahl 1995). Remittances also benefit individual recipients by raising and maintaining living standards and reducing the gap between higher-income and lower-income groups (Menjivar et al. 1998; Russell 1986). There is also evidence from many Pacific Island countries that remittances form a significant part of disposable household income (Connell 1980; Appleyard and Stahl 1995). For example, a national income and expenditure survey in Tonga showed that 90 percent of the households received remittances and that remittances constituted an average of 28 percent of household income (Ahlburg 1991; Brown 1998).

1

Because of the importance of remittances, policy makers are concerned with the long-term sustainability of these flows. Migrant remittance theory, however, predicts the level of remittances sent by migrants will decline through time. The "remittance decay" hypothesis modeled by Stark (1978) suggests that individual remittances will peak soon after arrival and then decline, increasing occasionally in response to specific events or needs by relatives in the home country. Eventually, remittances will cease, increasing again only if the migrant decides to return home permanently. The concept of altruism is central to Stark's theory of remittance decay. In the remittance literature, altruism is generally defined as the concern migrants have for their non-migrant family members in their countries of origin. Stark attributes the decline in remittance behavior through time to the waning of altruism. As the migrants' commitment and attachment to their families and home areas weaken through time, remittances decline.

Although research on remittance decay is limited, much of it fails to support Stark's hypothesis. This is especially true when considering research on remittances in the Pacific. For example, research on the remittance behavior of Tongans and Cook Islanders in Australia and New Zealand found that the amount of money sent by recent migrants was similar to that remitted by migrants who had arrived 15 to 20 years earlier (Loomis 1990; Tongamoa 1987; Vete 1995). Also, research on the remittance behavior of Fijians in Australia suggests that length of residency overseas does not substantially affect remittance flows (Stanwix and Connell 1995). While the results of these studies are troubled by small sample sizes and rudimentary statistical techniques, a study by Brown (1998) using tobit regression and controls for a number of "supply" and "demand" side variables leads to much the same conclusion. Brown found that the passage of time did not have a significant effect on the remittance behavior of Tongans and Western Samoans in Australia.

A SOCIOLOGICAL APPROACH TO MIGRANT REMITTANCES

The lack of support exhibited by the results of empirical research for remittance theory raises an interesting question: If remittances do not decline, as suggested by the remittance decay hypothesis, why do they continue through time, as suggested by the results of research on Pacific Island migrant populations? And if it is true that altruism, as a motive for remitting, wanes through time, what causes the commitment to remit to be sustained?

In this research, I use migrant network theory and the concepts of social capital and the strength of social ties to develop an alternative sociological framework to help answer these questions. This sociological approach suggests alternative explanations of what remittances are, why they occur, and why they decay – or endure – through time. Remittances are not the by-product of the altruism a migrant feels for his or her family. Rather, they are the resources exchanged between members of a migrant social network. Remittances occur as the result of migrants' participation in these networks and represent the migrants' effort to build and maintain social capital. Social capital refers to the ability of individuals to obtain resources through their continued relationships with other network members. Within these networks, both migrants and non-migrants act as donors and recipients of social capital, making their resources available to network members while simultaneously accessing the resources of others. Remittances are not simply "sent" by the migrant to family members back home but are exchanged for resources accessible through the maintenance of relationships with other members of a given social network.

In the remittance literature, it is generally assumed that migrants are directly motivated to remit by, for example, their altruistic feelings for family members or their own self-interest. However, viewing remittances as part of a migrant's effort to build and maintain social capital makes the link between the occurrence of remittances and the motivation to remit less direct. Remittances occur because the migrant has established and is maintaining a relationship with another member of a social network. In other words, relationships come first, and the motivation to remit comes after, not the other way around. Without relationships, there would be no remittances. Instead of asking what motivates a migrant to remit, this research focuses on those factors that enable a migrant to maintain the relationship in which remittances are exchanged.

Strong Kin Ties, Family Reunification Migration, and Remittance Decay

Recognizing the social basis on which remittance behavior is based is fundamental to understanding why remittances endure or decay through time. According to remittance research, the majority of the migrant/non-migrant relationships in which remittances are exchanged are immediate kin ties, including spouses, children, parents, and siblings. Because strong kin ties form the basis of remittance behavior, remittances will continue as long as those relationships are maintained through time. Remittance decay reflects the gradual change and ending of those ties maintained by household members with immediate kin in the country of origin.

In this research, I argue that the migration process, specifically family reunification migration, is the underlying social process that determines the remittance behavior of migrant households. The results of the analyses are consistent with this posited association between family reunification and remittance behavior. They show a negative association between the point in time the household received its last migrant member and the probability of remitting. This suggests that households in the middle of the family reunification process are the most active remitters. The results also indicate that households with a history of family reunification are more likely to remit. This suggests that family reunification has a positive influence on remittance behavior. Combined with the results of qualitative research on the remittance behavior of Pacific Island migrants, these results suggest a possible reason why remittances rise and decay through time. Remittance levels increase as the migrant household works to support dependent family members in the country of origin and to assist in their eventual migration. As the process of family reunification is gradually completed, fewer and fewer immediate kin remain overseas and remittance levels begin to decline. When the last migrant joins the household and all of the dependent family members have joined the earliest migrant overseas, the flow of remittances sent back home ends. Thus, the time path for remittance behavior is largely driven by the process of family reunification.

Migrant Network Theory and Remittance Duration

The influence of the migration process not only explains why remittances decline, but why they continue through time. Households will continue remitting as long as their migrant members have dependent relatives overseas. Migrant network theory suggests a second way remittance behavior is maintained through time. The active and continued participation by household members in migrant networks helps to promote remittance behavior by maintaining the relationships between migrants and non-migrants. Migrant networks are sets of interpersonal ties that connect migrants, former migrants, and non-migrants in origin and destination countries through ties of kinship, friendship, and shared national origins. Networks reduce the costs and disruptions of migration, maintain links between sending and receiving communities, serve as channels for information and resources, and influence the rate of adaptation and assimilation to the destination society (Massey et al. 1987).

Network participation can reduce the migrants' rate of adaptation and assimilation into the wider receiving community. This is significant for remittance behavior for three reasons. First, network participation can maximize the number of social links the migrants maintain with members of the society of origin. Heavy reliance on migrant networks means the migrants' personal social networks will be dominated by ties with other co-ethnics. Second, network participation can minimize the number of social links migrants establish with members of the receiving society. In this way, networks serve to insulate migrants from non-members. Third, network participation encourages the inter-dependence of network members in the country of destination. This can lead to the re-establishment of behavioral norms overseas and a heightened orientation towards the culture and society of origin.

By slowing the rate of adaptation and assimilation to the destination society, network participation maximizes the links with and orientation to the society of origin and insulates the migrants from the broader community. This indirectly encourages migrants to maintain their relationships with their non-migrant relatives overseas. By helping to maintain these relationships, migrants who are active network members will be encouraged to remit. As the results of the analyses will show, network participation by migrant household members does have a positive influence on remittance behavior, which suggests that network participation reinforces remittance behavior. However, there is little evidence to suggest that household network participation has any influence on the relationship between time and remittance behavior.

PURPOSE OF RESEARCH

The goal of this research is to examine the influence of time on remittance behavior and to provide an explanation of why some migrant communities maintain high levels of remittances over long periods, while in others significant remittance behavior never occurs. In this study, I will analyze the influence of continued and family reunification migration and network participation on household remittance behavior. I hypothesize that households reconstituted overseas through a process of family reunification migration will be more likely to remit than will households whose members migrated at the same time. I also hypothesize that households whose members participate in migrant networks will be more likely to remit and will remit at higher levels than will households whose members have isolated themselves from the migrant networks. In this study, I use logistic and OLS regression and data from the Census of Micronesian Migrants to Hawaii and Guam to examine the remittance behavior of migrant households from the Federated States of Micronesia, an island country in the north Pacific. By focusing on the processes that influence the motivation and ability of migrants to maintain their relationships with non-migrants, the empirical results of this research will work to resolve the contradictory findings regarding the decay and maintenance of remittances through time.

Main Findings

The main findings of this research include the following:

1. When remittance behavior is modeled at the household level, the results provide support for the remittance decay hypothesis.
2. Remittances reflect the process of household reconstitution overseas, specifically family reunification migration. Family reunification is the underlying social process driving remittance duration and decay.
3. Time works indirectly on household remittance behavior, especially the probability of remitting, through the process of continued migration. Time is more significant for those households reconstituting overseas through family reunification than for those households whose members migrated simultaneously.
4. Network participation has a positive influence on the likelihood that a household will remit, as well as the level of remittances sent overseas. However, it has no influence on the relationship between time and remittance behavior.

CHAPTER 2

A Sociological Model of Remittance Behavior

Since the 1970s, migrant remittance research has been dominated by economic theories and hypotheses. In general, this economic approach has focused on placing the remittance behavior of migrants into the context of both the household migration decision-making process as well as the household's effort to minimize financial risk and maximize long-term income stability. Remittances are seen as the resources sent by migrants to non-migrant household members to fulfill the contractual obligations incurred prior to migrating. This economic approach acknowledges the influence that the household context has on individual-level behavior, including remittance behavior. However, it fails to account for the influence that the migration process has on both the behavior of those households as well as their individual members. This is significant, because the migration process, by putting space – both time and distance – between household members, alters both the structure of the household as a social unit and the nature of the relationships maintained between migrant and non-migrant family members. As I argue below, in order to understand and explain remittance behavior, it is first necessary to acknowledge the primacy of the relationships between migrant sender and non-migrant receiver and then to analyze the influence that the migration process has on those relationships. Rather than focusing primarily on the economic role that remittances play in the lives of migrants and their families, this research takes a decidedly sociological approach to remittance behavior, focusing instead on the ability of migrants to maintain the relationships in which remittances are exchanged.

This chapter begins with a review of the economic theory that has dominated remittance research. This review focuses on answering the key questions that have motivated much of remittance research, including: Why do migrants remit? How are remittances enforced or ensured? Will remittances continue through time? The review also summarizes the results of remittance research and demonstrates how many of the hypotheses generated from economic theory, including the remittance decay hypothesis, have received mixed support from the empirical analyses. The lack of support exhibited by the empirical research suggests the need for an alternative framework to study remittance behavior. The second section of this chapter describes such a framework. It begins with a review of several sociological theories and concepts not traditionally used in remittance research. These include the concept of social capital, migrant network theory, and the concept of the strength of social ties. Each of these theories and concepts contributes to the development of an analytical framework that provides alternative *sociological* answers to the same key questions addressed in the remittance literature. Based on this analytical framework, the final section of this chapter describes the specific questions and hypotheses addressed in later chapters.

MIGRANT REMITTANCE THEORY AND THE REMITTANCE DECAY HYPOTHESIS

The remittance decay hypothesis, first formulated in the late 1970s (Stark 1978), is part of a larger body of work on remittance behavior by Stark and his colleagues (Katz and Stark 1986; Lucas and Stark 1985; Rosenweig and Stark 1989; Stark 1978, 1980, 1985; Stark and Bloom 1985; Stark and Levhari 1982; Stark and Lucas 1988; Stark and Taylor 1989; Stark, Taylor and Yitzhaki 1986). Much of this work and work by other researchers (Poirine 1997) on remittance behavior addresses three questions. First, what motivates a migrant to remit? Second, how are migrant remittances enforced or ensured? Third, will remittances continue through time? Table 2-1 summarizes the major theories and hypotheses that have guided remittance research since the late 1970s.

Stark and his colleagues view remittances as the result of risk avoidance and investment. In an economy where insurance and credit markets are underdeveloped, migration can be seen as a diversification response in the face of risk. Households intentionally allocate their members to geographically dispersed and structurally different labor markets to minimize risk and maximize income. This reduces the risk of losing income in individual markets and stabilizes income for all members of a household. Migrants remit because of an "implicit co-insurance contractual agreement" that exists between the migrant and his/her family in the area of origin. The family invests its resources in the migrant's education and reduces the risk associated with migrating by paying the cost of transportation and settlement and guaranteeing the migrant a minimum level of income during periods of unemployment. In exchange, once stable employment and income are obtained, the migrant agrees to remit a portion of his/her earnings, insuring a regular income for the family and providing the household with capital for risky investments. Remittances can be seen as both a return on investment in the migrant's education and as the delayed payment of a premium for the insurance provided by the family during the period of establishment and unemployment. At various times throughout the migration process, the migrant and family act as "insurer" and "insured," with remittances as claims flowing to the family in times of need and to the migrant during periods of unemployment.

Viewing remittances as part of an implicit contract raises the question of enforcement. Because the contract is voluntary it must be self-enforcing. Stark suggests two reasons why the co-insurance contract is self-enforcing: 1) mutual altruism and 2) tempered altruism/enlightened self-interest. In the remittance literature, altruism usually refers to the concern that a migrant has for the well being of his/her family left behind. For example, it is generally believed that one of the main reasons migrants remit is because of altruistic feelings they have for their families back home. The mutual altruism that exists among the migrant and non-migrant

Table 2-1: Summary of Migrant Remittance Theories and Hypotheses

Theory/Hypothesis and Author(s)	Summary
New Economics of Migration Stark and Bloom (1985)	*Question:* **Why does migration occur?** Migration decisions are made by groups of related persons, typically families or households, who work together to develop economic strategies that maximize household earnings and minimize risks to their financial well being. When compared to developed countries, risk is attenuated for households in less developed countries because of characteristics associated with developing economies. In developed economies, institutional mechanisms (e.g., private insurance markets, government insurance programs) exist that can minimize risk to household incomes. There are also developed credit markets that provide families with the capital necessary to finance new projects. In developing economies, these institutional mechanisms are non-existent, underdeveloped, or inaccessible to many families, especially poor families. In the absence of other ways to insure themselves against risk, households use migration to allocate family members to geographically dispersed and structurally different labor markets, thereby reducing the overall risk to family income. Assuming the rural and urban/foreign economies are weakly or negatively correlated, the household can rely on migrant remittances for support if the local economy should deteriorate and income decline. During periods of economic stability, these remittances can also be used for capital accumulation, thereby circumventing the need for establish credit markets.
The Implicit Co-Insurance Contractual Agreement Approach Stark and Lucas (1988)	*Question:* **Why do migrants remit?** Remittances are the resources exchanged between migrant and non-migrant members of a household and are the result of the household's attempt to maximize the stability of long-term income. Migrants remit because an implicit co-insurance contractual agreement exists between a migrant and home. Two elements of this agreement are investment and risk. The family invests resources in the health and education of a perspective migrant. When the person migrates, the family reduces the risk involved with the move by paying for the cost of transportation and guaranteeing a minimum level of income until the migrant is established. Remittances

Table 2-1: Summary of Migrant Remittance Theories and Hypotheses *(Continued)*

Theory/Hypothesis and Author(s)	Summary
	can be seen as both a return on investment in the migrant's education and as the delayed payment of a premium for the insurance provided by the family during the period of establishment and unemployment. Once stable employment and income are secured, the migrant is expected to become the insurer by sending remittances back home. Remittances insure a regular income for the family and help non-migrant family members cover the premiums necessary to make risky investments in the home economy. Remittances as claims would flow to the family in times of need and to the migrant during periods of unemployment. By exchanging risks when the other is in a relatively less risky state, both are able to undertake activities that are highly risky in the short run.
Mutual Altruism Lucas and Stark (1985) Stark and Lucas (1988)	*Question:* **How are remittances enforced? Why is the co-insurance contract self-enforcing?** Altruism refers to the concern that a migrant has for the well being of the family left behind. However, altruism is not simply uni-directional, from migrant to family. Rather, members of a family, both migrant and non-migrant, have feelings of mutual altruism towards one another. Mutual altruism generates an effect similar to trust or loyalty among family members. This trust or loyalty helps to reinforce adherence to a contract, such as an agreement to remit, which reduces the need for costly contractual safeguards. Mutual altruism also assists family members in solving problems that emerge when legally enforced property rights and contingent contracts cannot be written. By increasing the self-enforceability of the contract, the altruism that exists among family members makes a migrant-family contractual arrangement more cost efficient than alternative, non-family contractual arrangements. Thus, the migrant and family have an incentive to turn to one another even when alternative parties exist. By entering into an agreement with each other, family members are relatively assured about the fulfillment of contractual provisions.

Table 2-1: Summary of Migrant Remittance Theories and Hypotheses *(Continued)*

Theory/Hypothesis and Author(s)	Summary
Tempered Altruism/ Enlightened Self-Interest Lucas and Stark (1985) Stark and Lucas (1988)	*Question*: **How are remittances enforced? Why is the co-insurance contract self-enforcing?** A migrant's altruism towards the family back home is tempered by self-interest, that is, there is an element of self-interest in honoring the contract. Self-interest not only refers to the benefits the migrant derives from complying with the implicit contract but to other benefits as well. Factors such as the desire to inherit, the need to maintain rural investments, and the intention to eventually return home means that the migrant retains a vested interest in his/her origins beyond altruistic concerns. While the migrant may have ultimate control over the decision to remit, the family back home may also have control over resources in which the migrant has a vested interest. This interest increases the family's confidence that the migrant will not default on his/her remittance payments which, in turn, encourages adherence to and increases the self-enforceability of the co-insurance contract.
The Remittance Decay Hypothesis Stark (1978); Stark and Lucas (1988)	*Question*: **Will remittances continue through time?** This model links remittance levels, a migrant's home commitment, and the length of urban residence. Remittances sent by a migrant will peak soon after arrival and then decline, increasing occasionally in response to specific events or needs by relatives in the home area. Eventually, remittances will cease, increasing again only if the migrant decides to return home permanently. Initially, remittances are low but increase with time as the migrant adjusts to the new urban environment and is relieved of the initial costs associated with migration and settlement. Eventually, as the migrant's urban perception of rural needs and attachments to the rural area weakens, remittances decline. Altruism is key to understanding remittance behavior. The waning of the migrant's altruism would weaken the self-enforcing property of the migrant-family contractual agreement. A migrant may cease to send remittances if the arrangement is no longer self-enforcing.

members of a household generates an effect similar to trust or loyalty among family members. This trust or loyalty helps to reinforce the adherence to the provisions of a contract, such as an agreement to remit, which reduces the need for costly contractual safeguards. By entering into an agreement with each other, family members are relatively assured about the fulfillment of contractual provisions. This makes contracts among family members more self-enforceable and therefore more cost efficient than alternative, non-family arrangements.

A second reason why the co-insurance contract is self-enforcing is tempered altruism or enlightened self-interest. A migrant's altruism towards his/her family back home is tempered by self-interest. Self-interest not only refers to the benefits the migrant derives from complying with the implicit contract but to other benefits as well. Factors such as the desire to inherit, the need to maintain rural investments, or the intention to eventually return home means that the migrant retains a vested interest in his/her origins beyond altruistic concerns. While the migrant may have ultimate control over the decision to remit, the family back home may also have control over resources in which the migrant has a vested interest (e.g., land, a home, cattle, etc.). This interest increases the family's confidence that the migrant will not default on his/her remittance payments which, in turn, encourages adherence to and increases the self-enforceability of the co-insurance contract.

The Remittance Decay Hypothesis

According to Stark, altruism is key to understanding remittance behavior. As one clause in the co-insurance agreement, remittances are ensured not just by the benefits the contract offers to both migrant and family but also by the altruism-generated reinforcement mechanisms that increase the probability of compliance. This raises the question: Will the remittance behavior of migrants be short or long term? That is, will remittances continue through time? Commenting on the nature of altruism, Stark and Lucas (1988: 469) state that "it is perhaps reasonable to assume that, in general, altruism will wane through time."[i] This waning of the migrant's altruism would weaken the self-enforcing property of the migrant-family contractual agreement. A migrant may cease to send remittances if the arrangement is no longer self-enforcing.

In an earlier work on rural-to-urban migration and development, Stark (1978) proposed a model which links remittance levels, a migrant's home "commitment," and the length of urban residence. Known as the "remittance decay" hypothesis, Stark suggests that the remittances sent by individual migrants will peak soon after arrival and then decline, increasing occasionally in response to specific events or needs by relatives in the home area. Eventually, remittances will cease, increasing again only if the migrant decides to return home permanently. Initially, remittances are low but increase with time as the migrant adjusts to his/her new urban environment and is relieved of the initial costs associated with moving to a new area. Eventually, as the migrant's urban perception of rural needs and attachments to the rural area weakens, remittances decline. Stark argues that remittances vary with time for two reasons. First, because of the "impact of the intensity and nature of kinship relations, cohesion and social control" (Stark 1978:37) and, second, because of the changing economic status of the migrant. Combined, these two factors produce an inverse, bell-shaped functional relationship between remittances and time (see figure 2-1).

Empirical Support for Stark's Migrant Remittance Theories and Hypotheses

While the theories of remittance behavior by Stark and his colleagues provide an analytical framework to guide research, many of the hypotheses generated from this work have received mixed support from the results of empirical analyses. Table 2-2 summarizes the results from research that both supports and fails to support Stark's work. As can be seen by this brief review, the results of the empirical research neither completely supports nor refutes the various hypotheses put forth by Stark and his colleagues. For the most part, there is little or mixed evidence for a number of Stark's ideas, including remittances as a return for the investment in a migrant's education and tempered altruism/enlightened self-interest, while other views, such as remittances as insurance, receive

Figure 2-1:   Stark's Remittance Decay Curve

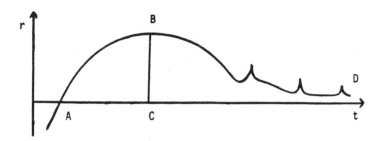

"The probable general relationship between net urban-to-rural remittances (measured in absolute terms at fixed prices) r and time t is schematically portrayed [above]: ABC – mainly when the migrant returns (or is joined by his family). ABD – when he does not return; the sporadical pattern of BD reflects remittances in response to acute needs or special events at the rural end (e.g., marriage of a sibling, a festival)" (Stark 1978:37).

limited but positive support. While there is little support for a purely altruistic motive of remittances, there is support for Stark's concept of mutual altruism. It appears that the trust or loyalty generated by the mutual altruism among migrant and non-migrant family members encourages remittances to be directed towards close family members, including spouses, children, parents, and siblings. While the support for tempered altruism/enlightened self-interest is questionable, research does indicate that pure self-interest motivates remittance behavior. The desire to eventually return home, to start a new business, pursue political aspirations, or retire has a positive influence on remittance behavior.

Remittance Decay – or Duration?

According to the remittance decay hypothesis, the frequency and amount of remittances should decline through time as the migrant's commitment to his/her family and area of origin weakens. However, most research on remittance behavior has failed to find a negative association between time and remittances. For example, research on the remittance behavior of

Table 2-2: Summary of Support for Hypotheses Derived from Migrant Remittance Theories

Hypothesis	Research That Fails to Support Hypothesis	Research That Supports Hypothesis	Conclusion
Altruism	Brown (1998), Lucas and Stark (1985), Oberai and Singh (1980)	Banerjee (1984), Brown (1998), Funkhouser (1995), Johnson and Whitelaw (1974), Knowles and Anker (1981), Macpherson (1994), Menjivar et al. (1998), Rempel and Lobdell (1978)	There is little evidence in the literature to support the existence of altruistic motives in remittance behavior. Most research has failed to find a negative association between the income of the family of origin and the amount of remittances received. However, research clearly demonstrates that the majority of remittances are sent to close relatives (e.g., parents, spouse, children, siblings) and that the presence of close relatives in the area of origin strongly influences both the decision to remit and the amount remitted.
Remittances as Insurance	--	Lucas and Stark (1985), Ravallion and Dearden (1988), Stark and Lucas (1988)	There is evidence to support the view that remittances are a form of insurance among migrant and non-migrant family members during times of need. Remittances increase to rural families during periods of drought, and illness and to urban migrants during periods of unemployment.
Remittances as Investment	Banerjee (1984), Brown (1998), Funkhouser (1992), Hoddinott (1992)	Lucas and Stark (1985), Knowles and Anker (1981), Rempel and Lobdell (1978), Stark and Lucas (1988)	There is mixed support for the view that remittances represent repayment for the investment made in the migrant's education. Earlier research provided some indirect support, but was criticized for its failure to deal with issues of sample selection and censoring. Later research generally fails to support the view of remittances as repayment for education.

Table 2-2: Summary of Support for Hypotheses Derived from Migrant Remittance Theories *(Continued)*

Hypothesis	Research That Fails to Support Hypothesis	Research That Supports Hypothesis	Conclusion
Tempered Altruism/ Enlightened Self-Interest	Brown (1998), Rempel and Lobdell (1978)	Hoddinott (1992), Johnson and Whitelaw (1974), Lucas and Stark (1985)	There is mixed support for tempered altruism/enlightened self-interest. Most of the studies that support this view use only indirect measures, and many have been criticized for failing to deal with issues of sample selection and censoring. The only study using direct measures (Brown 1998) fails to find any support for tempered altruism/enlightened self-interest.
Pure Self-Interest	---	Brown (1998), Ahlburg and Brown (1998), Macpherson (1994)	Research has found that migrants who intend to return to their country of origin will remit more than migrants who intend to stay. These studies support the view that remittances are driven in part by self-interest and the accumulation of assets (both financial and social) rather than only by altruism and the need for family consumption support.
Remittance Decay	Banerjee (1984), Brown (1998), Funkhouser (1995), Loomis (1990), Lucas and Stark (1985), Oberai and Singh (1980), Tongamoa (1987), Vete (1995).	Funkhouser (1995), Knowles and Anker (1981) Lucas and Stark (1985), Menjivar et al. (1998)	The majority of research on remittances that include a duration variable in their regression equations conclude that remittances do not decline through time, but there are studies that support the remittance decay hypothesis. Many of these studies, however, are based on small samples, fail to correct for sample selection and censoring issues, and use duration variables that lack sufficient depth. The only study to formally test the remittance decay hypothesis (Brown 1998) finds no evidence of a downward sloping remittance function.

Tongans and Cook Islanders in Australia and New Zealand shows that the amount of money sent by recent migrants was similar to that remitted by migrants who had arrived 15 to 20 years earlier (Loomis 1990; Tongamoa 1987; Vete 1995). Also, Oberai and Singh (1980) find that the proportion of Indian rural-to-urban migrants remitting to their families actually increased through time. However, as Brown (1998:113) notes, all of these studies are based on small samples that cannot be considered statistically reliable. They also use cross-tabulation analysis that cannot isolate the effects of other variables from the effect of duration of absence.

Unlike the generally consistent results derived from cross-tabulation analysis, research relying on ordinary least-squares regression has produced conflicting results regarding the association between time and remittances. Lucas and Stark (1985) find that remittances continue to rise in the first five years away from home, but then decline. However, Stark and Lucas (1988) find a pattern of remittance behavior that indicates a "dwindling rise" rather than a decline in remittances through time. Knowles and Anker (1981) find a negative association between the years of residence away from home and the decision to remit, indicating that a migrant's obligation to remit weakens through time. However, they find no relationship between the years spent away from home and the amount remitted, indicating time has no influence on the amount of money sent overseas. This is supported by the results of Menjivar et al. (1998). Using a combination of logit and OLS regression, they find that the number of years in the United States negatively influences the decision to remit but has no influence on the amount remitted. Thus, there appears to be some evidence when the passage of time influences remittance behavior, it affects the decision to remit rather than the amount remitted.

Modeling remittance behavior using a combination of either probit or logit and OLS regression allows the researcher to analyze separately the influence of variables on the probability of remitting and on the amount remitted. First, probit or logit analysis is used to determine the likelihood of remitting and then OLS regression is used to determine the influence of variables on the amount remitted. A number of researchers prefer to use tobit regression analysis, which enables the researcher to model the influence that variables have on the likelihood of remitting and the amount remitted in a single equation. Banerjee (1984) uses both probit/OLS and tobit regression to analyze data on internal remittances in India. While the models demonstrate some differences in the significance levels of the years of urban residence variables, Banerjee concludes that the analyses show no evidence of a decline in remittances through time. However, Banerjee's duration variable only spanned twelve years, which may not be a long enough period for a remittance pattern to be well established. Funkhouser (1995) also uses probit/OLS and tobit regression to analyze the remittance behavior of Salvadoran and Nicaraguan migrants in the United States. While his models also demonstrate some differences in the significance of the years since emigration variables, Funkhouser concludes that increases in the years since emigration are associated with lower remittances. He also finds a significant interaction between the years since emigration and whether or not the migrant was a family member of a Salvadoran household. The results show that non-family members are less likely to remit and remit less than family members, while family members continue to remit through time. However, the mean years since emigrating for both the Salvadoran and Nicaraguan samples are approximately six years, which may not be a long enough period for a remittance decay pattern to be established.

To date, only Brown (1998) explicitly tests the remittance decay hypothesis using tobit regression analysis. In addition to the duration variables (length of absence and its square), Brown includes "demand-side," "supply-side," and "behavioral or motivational" variables. Demand-side variables include those factors associated with the country of origin that put pressure on the migrant from the receiving end, such as the presence of close family members overseas. Supply-side variables influence a migrant's capacity to remit, such as income. Behavioral variables include those characteristics that influence a migrant's motivation to remit, such as whether the migrant considers his or her parents to be poor or expects to inherit assets from a parent living in the country of origin. Unlike Banerjee (1984) and Funkhouser (1995), the duration variables Brown uses span over 20 years. Because the duration variables are not statistically significant, Brown concludes that there is no evidence that the remittance functions of migrants are downward sloping as predicted by the remittance decay hypothesis.

A SOCIOLOGICAL APPROACH TO REMITTANCE DURATION AND DECAY

In most studies to date, there is little support for the remittance decay hypothesis. In fact, some research on remittance behavior, especially research on Pacific Island migrant populations, suggests that remittances continue through time. If remittances do not represent repayment for loans foisted upon young, unsuspecting migrants-to-be by the rational, calculating members of their natal households, what do they represent? What motivates a migrant to remit? And if it is true that altruism, as a motive for remitting, wanes through time, what causes the commitment to remit to be sustained? Based on the concepts of risk, investment, and insurance, economists have suggested a number of theories and hypotheses that provide answers to these questions. However, empirical research has provided most of these theories and hypotheses with mixed support. Perhaps a better explanation of remittance behavior can be developed by emphasizing the social – rather than economic – role that remittances play in the lives of migrants and their families. Although network theory does not directly address remittance behavior, research focusing on social and migrant networks and on the concept of social capital, when combined, suggest alternative reasons why migrants remit, how remittances are enforced, and why they are maintained through time. They also suggest reasons why remittance behavior decays through time.

The Concept of Social Capital

As generally defined by the literature, social capital refers to the resources embedded in social networks that are available to individuals through their relations with other network members (Bordieu 1986; Coleman 1988; Lin 2001; Portes 1998; Portes and Sessenbrenner 1993). Social capital is analogous to the better-known concept of human capital (Lin 2001).

According to human-capital theory, individuals invest in improving their technical skills and knowledge, for example, by obtaining a college education, to obtain an expected return, such as higher pay for their labor. In social capital theory, individuals invest in social relations, by interacting and networking with others, in order to gain access to resources embedded in the network and to produce some benefit or profit. In this sense, social capital is more than simply the resources in a network, but refers to the ability of individuals to use their social relations with others to gain access to those resources for their own use.

One of the advantages of social capital theory is its ability to use both social structure and rational action in explaining individual behavior (Coleman 1988). Traditionally, sociology has viewed the actor as socialized and action as governed by social norms, rules, and obligations. Emphasis has been placed on the social context and using that context to explain the way action is shaped, constrained, and redirected. In contrast, economics has viewed the actor as independent and action determined by rational, independently derived goals achieved in a wholly self-interested fashion. While the sociological approach has been criticized for "over-socializing" action, denying the actor agency, or the ability to define and execute purposive action, the economic approach has been criticized for ignoring the influence of social structure on individual behavior (*see* Coleman 1989:S95-S97). By comparison, social capital theory combines the strength of both these traditions, overcoming these criticisms. It provides agency to individual actors by acknowledging their efforts in the development, maintenance, and use of social relations to obtain resources for their own benefit. At the same time, it recognizes that actors have positions in social networks and that social networks themselves have limited resources, both of which shape, redirect, and constrain action.

One way social networks can influence the amount of social capital available to its members is through closure. Closure refers to the existence of a sufficient number, or density, of ties among a group of people that ensures the observance of norms (Portes 1998). Coleman (1988) argues that closure is advantageous to network members because it helps maintain and enhance trust, norms, authority, sanctions, etc. that can be used by individuals to mobilize network resources. In this way, social capital is created by the strongly interconnected members of a social network. Lin (2001) argues that denser networks may have a relative advantage for preserving and maintaining the resources a network already has. However, for searching for and obtaining resources not available within a network, accessing and extending "bridges" to other social networks should be more useful. Burt (1992) has argued that these bridges, or "structural holes," between otherwise separate networks facilitate individual action. This is because the connection an actor would have with other members of a dense, closed network would likely convey redundant information, whereas weaker ties with members of other social networks can be sources of new knowledge and resources.

Migrant Remittances and Social Capital

What are remittances? According to the concept of social capital (Bordieu 1986; Coleman 1988; Lin 2001; Portes 1998; Portes and Sesenbrenner 1993), remittances are the resources exchanged between members of a social network. A social network, in its most general sense, is a structured set of social relationships among individuals (Lomnitz 1976). Social networks provide their members with relationships that allow them access to the resources possessed by other members of their networks, including remittances. However, remittances are more than simply resources exchanged by network members because they represent a migrant's effort to build and maintain social capital. Social capital refers to the ability of individuals "to secure benefits by virtue of membership in social networks or other social structures" (Portes 1998:6). Relative to other forms of capital, social capital has an intangible character. While "economic capital is in people's bank accounts and human capital is inside their heads, social capital inheres in the structure of their relationships" (Portes 1998:7). To possess social capital, an individual must have relationships with others. It is these relationships with others, and not the resources or abilities possessed by the individual, that matters most.

When considering the concept of social capital, it is important to distinguish the resources available within a social network from the ability of individuals to obtain these resources through membership. Portes (1998:6) argues that any systematic treatment of the concept of social capital must distinguish among 1) the possessors of social capital (those making claims to resources), 2) the sources of social capital (those agreeing to these demands) and 3) the resources themselves. In the context of remittance behavior, migrants who remit to their families are the source of social capital, while their family members who request and receive remittances are the possessors of social capital. Remittances are the resources exchanged between donors and recipients and are the result of the continuing relationships between the migrant and non-migrant members of a network.

Social Capital as the Motivation for Remittance Behavior

The concept of social capital as detailed by Portes (1998; Portes and Sesenbrenner 1993) suggests what remittances are and why they exist. Remittances are not a by-product of the altruism a migrant feels for his/her family. Rather, remittances are the resources exchanged among the members of a social network. However, remittances are more than simply resources. They also represent the migrant's effort to build and maintain social capital. Specifically, migrants as donors act as the sources of social capital, supplying remittances to those who request them, while their non-migrant family members act as the possessors of social capital, making claims to those resources. Migrants also act as the possessors of social capital, making claims on the resources of their families' back home, which explains why remittances are bi-directional.

What motivates the migrant donors to respond to their families' needs and requests by remitting resources back home? The concept of social capital also suggests how remittance behavior is ensured. Three types of social capital – value introjection, reciprocity exchanges, and enforceable trust – are especially useful in explaining what motivates donors to make their resources available to other members of their networks. These motives are clearly demonstrated in the sociological and anthropological research on Pacific Island cultures.

Value introjection refers to an individual's obligation to behave in a certain manner that arises out of values learned during the process of socialization. People pay their bills, stop at red lights, and care for their elderly parents because it is what the "should" do. Internalized norms make such behavior possible and it is this behavior that can be appropriated by others as a resource. Many migrants are motivated to remit to their families back home because of value introjection. In addition to the money migrants remit to support their relatives overseas, migrants also remit airline tickets, sponsor new migrant relatives, pay the school tuition of younger relatives, send donations for village social events and development projects, and send money and materials to build a house for their parents because it is the "right thing to do" (Curson 1979; James 1997; Loomis 1990; MacPherson 1985, 1994; Small 1997; Vete 1995). These demands are not always easy for the migrants to fulfill and often entail personal sacrifices, such as taking a second job or living in or near poverty to maximize savings and remittances (Ahlburg 2000; Franco 1985; MacPherson 1985, 1994; Small 1997). However, this behavior is expected of them by their families and relatives – and by the migrants themselves – as overseas members of their villages and their communities (Curson 1979; Faeamani 1995; James 1991; Loomis 1990; Macpherson 1985, 1994; Shankman 1976; Stanwix and Connell 1995; Vete 1995).

The literature on remittance behavior also demonstrates that reciprocity exchanges are an important source of motivation for migrants, especially those from Pacific Island cultures. Reciprocity exchanges refer to the accumulation of obligations from others according to the norms of reciprocity. Donors provide privileged access to their resources in the expectation that they will be fully repaid in the future. Migrants remit cash and goods that are reciprocated by foodstuffs, handicrafts, and sometimes cash by their families back home (Curson 1979; Connell 1980; James 1991, 1997; Loomis 1990; Munro 1990; Small 1997; Stanwix and Connell 1995). While the monetary value of the foodstuffs and handicrafts remitted may at first seem nominal, many of these articles have great traditional value and are required for the proper execution of ceremonies, such as weddings and funerals. Reciprocity exchanges are also represented by "child-fostering" or "child-minding" arrangements (James 1991, 1997; see also Mattheai 1996 and Ho 1993). Parents who migrate will leave their children with relatives to be raised back home, thus reducing the cost of migration and living expenses overseas and ensuring their children will be raised in a traditional environment. In exchange, migrant parents remit money to support both their relatives and children. In this sense, the migrants are acting as recipients of social capital because they are accessing the child-fostering resources of their kin, even though it appears they are acting as donors by sending monetary resources to support their families back home.

Finally, enforceable trust refers to social capital generated by the compliance of individual members with group expectations. An individual is motivated by the anticipation of the benefits associated with maintaining a "good standing" within the group, so the internal monitoring and sanctioning capacity of the community plays an important role. The research literature on remittances in the Pacific has noted the importance of sanctions in ensuring that migrants will remit to their dependents back home (Connell 1980; Curson 1979; Macpherson 1994; Stanwix and Connell 1995; Vete 1995). Sanctions emphasize access to resources on the islands, such as land for housing, marital partners for the migrants or their children, the maintenance of family status, political authority, and investment opportunities. These sanctions are almost entirely related to future possibilities – possibilities that can be threatened by failure to demonstrate a commitment to their families, villages, and communities and maintain a "presence" in the islands through remittances (Connell 1980). Perhaps it is not surprising, then, that a number of studies have indicated that one of the main reasons migrants remit is to maintain their ability to return home in good standing with the community (Ahlburg and Brown 1998; Connell 1980; Macpherson 1994; Stanwix and Connell 1995). This is especially true for those migrants who maintain political aspirations back home and whose status, both individual and familial, is important to their future in the islands (Macpherson 1994).

Explaining Remittance Duration: Migrant Network Theory

The concepts of social networks and social capital may help explain both why remittances occur and what motivates migrants to remit. Remittances occur as the result of migrants' participation in social networks and represent the migrants' effort to build and maintain social capital. Within these networks, both migrants and non-migrants act as donors and recipients of social capital, making their resources available to network members while simultaneously accessing the resources of others. Viewing remittances as the resources exchanged between donors and recipients helps make the willingness of migrants to remit to their families back home more understandable. Migrants, as donors and recipients of social capital, may be motivated to remit for reasons of value introjection, reciprocal exchange, or enforceable trust. Remittances are not simply "sent" by the migrant to non-migrant family members, but are exchanged for resources, both tangible and intangible, accessible through the maintenance of relationships with other members of a given social network.

Viewing remittances as part of a migrant's effort to maintain and build social capital alters the meaning of "motivation" as it is generally defined in remittance research. It is generally assumed that remittances occur because the migrant is motivated by feelings of altruism, self-interest, fear of risk, etc. When adopting a social capital approach to remittance behavior, the link between the occurrence of remittances and the motivation to remit becomes less direct. That is, remittances occur because the migrant has established and is maintaining a relationship with another member of the social network. Put simply, relationships come first, the motivation to remit comes after. Without relationships, there would be no remittances. Thus, instead of asking what motivates a migrant to continue to remit, we should be asking what enables a migrant to maintain the relationships in which remittances are exchanged. Migrant network theory can help explain how the relationships among migrants and non-migrants are maintained and, in turn, help explain why remittances endure – or decay – through time.

A migrant network is a specialized kind of social network. Migrant networks are sets of interpersonal ties based on kinship, friendship, and shared nationality that connect migrants, former migrants, and non-migrants in origin and destination areas (Massey et al. 1993), and as such they represent an important source of social capital (Portes 1995). Migrant networks also serve many important functions for individual migrants, such as reducing the costs and disruptions of migration, maintaining links between sending and receiving communities, serving as channels for information and resources, and influencing the rate of adaptation and assimilation to the destination society (Gurak and Caces 1992). Migrant networks vary in their form and function, depending on the organizing principle underlying the network (e.g., reciprocal exchange), and they evolve over time and with the nurturing of relationships. The type of individuals sought for membership in the migrant network will depend on its organizing principle and on the resources and perceived needs of those already in the network (Gurak and Caces 1992:152). However, because the domestic unit is an important component in migrant networks, families and kin groups dominate its membership (Boyd 1989). This dominance reflects the constraints imposed by the nature of migration: "the weaker the ties connecting the points of a network, the harder it is to maintain the social arrangement as distance between the points increases" (Gurak and Caces 1992:152). Family and kin groups dominate migrant networks because they represent the social ties in a network that are strong enough to be maintained over time and distance.

Migrant network participation and remittance behavior

Migrant networks serve many important functions for their migrant members. However, when considering the influence that migrant network participation has on household remittance behavior, the most important of these functions is the influence that migrant networks have on the rate of adaptation and assimilation of their members to the destination society. Migrant networks can actually retard integration by maximizing links with and orientation towards the society of origin. This, in turn, should help maintain the relationships between migrants and non-migrants. This occurs in at least three ways. First, while migrant networks provide short-term adaptive assistance to recent migrants that can facilitate integration, such as finding housing, arranging employment, and providing emotional support, they can also insulate migrants from the destination society. Migrant networks strengthen the links migrants have to their sending society while effectively limiting contacts with the broader destination community (Gurak and Caces 1992). Heavy reliance on migrant networks for support means that ties with other co-ethnics dominate the immediate social networks of new migrants. This simultaneously maximizes the number and strength of ties with members of the origin society while minimizing the number of and the need for ties with members of the receiving society.

Second, kin groups tend to be the dominant social organization present in migrant networks and often represent the link between non-migrants in the country of origin and migrants in the country of destination that encourages continued migration through time (Boyd 1989; Gurak and Caces 1992; Massey et al. 1993). By guaranteeing that the social network of new migrants will be dominated by ties with relatives, migration under the auspices of kinship promotes the continuing intense involvement in kin groups (Tilly and Brown 1967; Gurak and Caces 1992). This reinforces the strength of ties to members of the origin society and slows the establishment of ties with members of the destination society, retarding integration and assimilation.

Finally, migrant networks can encourage the interdependence of network members in the country of destination that can lead, through time, to the establishment of migrant communities and the re-establishment of behavioral norms based on the culture of the community of origin (Grieco 1998). The participation in the wider migrant community provides migrants with culturally acceptable venues where additional ties to co-ethnics outside their immediate kin networks can be established and maintained. Also, participation in activities sponsored by the migrant community, such as ethnic organizations, sports associations, festivals, and ceremonies, not only provide venues for networking but also create "lacunae" in the wider host society where the migrants' cultural and behavioral norms can be both celebrated and reaffirmed. This helps strengthen and maintain the migrants' orientation to their origin society.

In these three ways, the continued participation by migrants in migrant networks maintains the bonds between migrants and non-migrants and encourages a continued orientation to the culture and society of origin. This reduces the migrants' rate of adaptation and assimilation to the destination society and, in turn, helps maintain remittance levels through time. Because the relationships between migrants and non-migrants form the social basis of remittance behavior, the fact that the continued participation in migrant networks encourages migrants to renew and maintain their relationships with non-migrants suggests it will also help maintain remittance levels through time. The cultural orientation engendered by migrant network participation should also have a positive influence on remittance behavior. Because migrant networks link migrants to their origin cultures, the same social sanctions that discourage reneging on commitments back home will have been transplanted into the migrant communities overseas. This cultural "pressure" will be reinforced by the interpersonal relationships established with other co-ethnics, which will act as constant reminders to the migrants' of their cultural obligations and duties to their families back home. This will encourage migrants who are active network members to maintain their relationships overseas and continue remitting.

Explaining Remittance Decay: The Strength of Social Ties

By helping to maintain the bonds between migrants and non-migrants, network theory suggests that the continued participation by migrants in migrant networks will have a positive influence on remittance behavior and will help maintain remittance levels through time. While network theory helps explain remittance duration, the concept of the strength of social ties (Granovetter 1973) can help explain why remittances decay through time. Among the members of a network, social ties can vary in strength of connection. According to Granovetter (1973:1,361), the strength of any tie is due to a combination of "the amount of time, the emotional intensity, the intimacy (mutual confiding), and the reciprocal services which characterize the tie." Strong ties include primary relationships, such as family and close friend relationships, that are based on important emotional linkages and/or frequent, routine interaction. Weak ties include relationships among individuals that lack the same emotional strength, such as among neighbors or co-workers. Granovetter argues that strong ties left unbalanced by weak ties result in the isolation of the network from broad segments of society. Weak ties are important because they unite diverse networks and increase the sources of resources available to network members.

In order to understand why remittances decline through time, it is first necessary to understand why research has found that remittances are exchanged almost exclusively between close relatives, including spouses, parents, children, and siblings (Connell and Brown 1995; Knowles and Anker 1981; MacPherson 1994; Stanwix and Connell 1995).[ii] There are two reasons for this. First, most of the relationships that survive the migration process and are maintained between migrants and non-migrants are strong kin ties. Strong ties are defined as relationships characterized by high contact frequency, emotional intensity, and reciprocal exchange (Wellman and Wortley 1990). Their maintenance requires the investment of considerable time and resources, so it is not surprising that the results of social networks research indicate that geographic distance and infrequent contact increase the difficulty of maintaining strong ties (Granovetter 1973; Wellman and Wortley 1990). By comparison, weak ties are relationships characterized by low contact frequency, emotional intensity, and reciprocal exchange and are, by extension, less likely to be maintained over space and time. In a study of community ties and social support in Toronto, Wellman and Wortley (1990) divide strong ties into two groups: strong ties based on friendships (i.e., strong ties) and strong ties based on relationships with relatives (i.e., strong kin ties). They found that ties with immediate kin do not depend on the strength or accessibility of those ties as much as other types of relationships do. Strong kin ties are much more likely to be maintained over time and space than either strong or weak ties.

Although their study did not specifically focus on migration, the results of Wellman and Wortley's (1990) research suggest why strong kin ties are more likely to survive the migration process than strong non-kin ties, weak kin ties, or weak non-kin ties. Migration, especially international migration, increases the geographic distance and reduces the contact frequency, emotional intensity, and reciprocal exchange between migrants and non-migrants. This separation will have a greater effect on weaker social ties than on stronger ones. The act of migrating will immediately eliminate all of an individual's weak ties, the majority of his/her strong ties, and many of his/her extended kin ties. Through time, because it is no longer possible to invest the amount of time or resources necessary to maintain strong ties based in the origin country, the majority – if not all – of the migrant's strong ties will disintegrate into weak ties and eventually disappear from his/her personal network. Also through time, many of the migrant's strong kin ties with peripheral family members will disintegrate into weak kin ties and be dropped from the migrant's personal network. The relationships most likely to survive migration, especially long-term or permanent migration, are the kin-based ties between the migrant and his/her immediate family members.

Social ties and resource exchange

Research by Wellman and Wortley (1990) also suggests a second reason why remittances are usually exchanged between close relatives. Remittances, including cash and in-kind exchanges, represent the type of social support commonly exchanged among immediate kin, but not among weak or strong ties or distant kin. Wellman and Wortley analyzed the relationship between different types of social ties and the kind of social support they offer to individuals. Specifically, they looked at five types of social support: 1) emotional aid and advice, 2) small services, 3) large services, 4) financial aid, and 5) companionship. Small services refer to minor services, such as lending or giving household items, minor household services, such assistance with minor repairs, and aid in dealing with organizations. Large services refer to major household services and repairs, regular services, such as reciprocal childcare services between in-laws, and major services, such as long-term health care. Financial aid includes large and small loans and gifts. In their analysis, Wellman and Wortley found differences among the types of social services associated with weak, strong, and kin ties. Strong ties provide broader support than weak ties, especially more emotional aid, minor services, and companionship, but also more large services and financial aid. However, it is immediate kin ties, and not strong ties, that are significantly associated with providing large services and financial aid. This is especially true among parents and children.

Wellman and Wortley (1990) also found that strong kin ties provide different resources than strong non-kin ties and that relatives, especially immediate family members, have distinct patterns in providing support. The parent and child roles are the most supportive of all role types. These roles provide all dimensions of support except for companionship. Siblings are similar to other strong friendship ties in that they provide emotional support and small services, but they are more likely to provide large services than are friends. Extended kin are the least likely of all network members to have provided any dimension of support. Immediate kin in general are less likely to be companions than are friends, but friends are often simply companions and do not provide any additional kind of support. The aid friends exchange depends on the strength of their relationship. However, unlike the support of friends, the availability of support from immediate kin is not conditional on the strength of the relationship. This may be because most of the respondents viewed their relationships with immediate kin in terms of long-term reciprocity.

The results of Wellman and Wortley's (1990) study shows that strong kin ties, especially parents and children, are the most likely of all social ties in a network to provide each other with financial aid and large services. This is significant for remittance research because many of the reasons why migrants send money home to their relatives – to support household consumption, to educate young family members, to assist in the migration of a relative, to build a house for their parents, to pay for child-fostering services – can easily be categorized as either financial aid or as support for the procurement of large services. The results of Wellman and Wortley's research suggest that, because close kin are most likely to provide one another with financial aid and large services, they are also the most likely migrant/non-migrant relationships to exchange remittances. Remittances are the type of social support provided by strong kin ties, and not by the weak or strong ties in a social network. Thus, strong kin ties form the basis of remittance behavior. This helps explain why migrants almost always exchange remittances with their immediate kin.

Changes in migrant/non-migrant relationships through time

The results of Wellman and Wortley's (1990) research, when applied to the migration process, help explain why remittances are exchanged most frequently between close relatives. Not only are strong kin ties the most likely of all relationships in a social network to survive the migration process, they are also the most likely relationships in which financial and service resources, including remittances, are exchanged. But how does this information help us understand why remittances decline through time? When considering possible reasons for remittance decay, it is first necessary to consider the nature of the relationships that form the basis of remittance behavior. Because the majority of the migrant/non-migrant relationships are strong kin ties, as indicated by both remittance and social network research, understanding the processes that alter the nature of those relationships should provide clues as to why remittances decay through time.

I argue that there are three ways that the strong kin relationship between migrants and non-migrants can be altered. First, non-migrants can join migrants overseas, thus dissolving the non-migrant status. Second, non-migrants can sever their dependent relationships on migrants through economic independence or by transferring their dependence to another non-migrant. Third, the migrant/non-migrant relationships can also be dissolved by death. Each of these changes, by altering the nature of the relationship between migrants and non-migrants, would end the exchange of remittances. Non-migrants who become migrants no longer receive remittances. Non-migrants who achieve economic independence or transfer their dependence to another non-migrant no longer require remittance support. Death, of course, ends the migrant/non-migrant relationship, which would also end remittance behavior. Thus, remittances will continue as long as the relationships between migrants and non-migrants 1) continue to exist and are not dissolved through migration or death and 2) maintain a social support function that includes the exchange of financial aid and, indirectly, large services. However, once the relationships between migrants and non-migrants end or the support function is nullified, remittances will also end.

Modeling household remittance decay

While the end of a relationship between a migrant and non-migrant can help explain why remittance behavior ends, it does not help explain why remittances would decay through time, as predicated by remittance theory (Stark 1978). I argue this is because the decay of remittances actually occurs at the household level rather than at the individual migrant/non-migrant relationship level. Because strong kin ties form the basis of remittance behavior, remittances will continue through time as long as the strong kin relationship between a migrant and non-migrant is maintained. Thus, at the individual level, remittance behavior will end when the strong kin relationship between a migrant and non-migrant ends. At the household level, however, remittances occur within a matrix of multiple strong kin ties. As with remittance behavior at the individual level, remittances will continue as long as those strong kin relationships are maintained. Also, the processes that change and end those strong kin ties remain the same as those discussed earlier: migration, economic independence, and death. But because there are multiple strong kin ties linking migrant household members with non-migrant relatives overseas, household remittance behavior will decay rather than abruptly end as those strong kin ties change and end, one by one, through time. In other words, remittance decay reflects the gradual change and ending of the strong kin ties maintained by household members with immediate relatives in the country of origin.

This process of household remittance decay is best illustrated by comparing the hypothetical influence that two common migration types would have on remittance behavior. This illustration will focus on two "models" of migration, including 1) family migration and 2) family chain migration. Family migration refers to the migration of a family unit, either a "family" as conventionally defined or a group of closely related persons, such as siblings or cousins. In the family migration model, it is assumed that all immediate family members migrate overseas at the same time and there is no additional migration of more distant kin or other non-relatives. Family chain migration refers to the continued migration of related persons to the same country of destination over a period of time. In this model, it is assumed that all non-migrants who join the household overseas are the immediate kin of the earlier migrants.

In family migration, the strong kin relationships in which remittances are most likely to be exchanged have all been reestablished in the country of destination. Households established through family migration will not remit because no strong kin ties remain in the country of origin. In family chain migration, strong kin relationships are separated between the countries of origin and destination. Chain-migrating households will continue to remit as long as the strong kin relationships between migrants and non-migrants remain separated in space and are maintained through time. Remittance decay only occurs in chain-migrating households. This is because the decay in remittance levels reflects the changing relative proportion of strong kin ties that exist in origin and destination countries through time. For example, in family chain migration, it is not unusual for one or a few family members to migrate overseas and establish a household "extension" with the express purpose of further family reunification. As the migrant household is established economically, remittance levels are initially low but quickly increase as household members work to support their immediate kin in the country of origin and to assist in their eventual migration. As the process of family reunification is gradually completed, fewer and fewer strong kin ties remain overseas and remittance levels peak and begin to decline. When the last migrant has joined the household and all the immediate family members have been reunited overseas, the flow of remittances back home will end.

This is not to say that all of the migrant family's strong kin ties will migrate and become part of the household overseas. During the period of family reunification overseas, many of those kin will have established themselves economically in the country of origin and will no longer require financial assistance or desire to migrate. This would occur, for example, if a migrant's sibling or child married and established a separate household. Other immediate kin may have transferred their dependence from the migrant household to other non-migrant households in the country of origin. This would occur, for example, if a migrant's elderly parents joined a sibling's household, making additional remittance support unnecessary. Other kin may have migrated elsewhere, using other channels of assistance. These processes, by eliminating the financial aid and large services support function of the migrant/non-migrant relationship, essentially equate the functions of strong kin ties with strong ties, thus abrogating the remittance responsibility of migrant households to those kin back home. Combined with family reunification migration and the death of non-migrant kin, these processes would reduce, and eventually eliminate, the number of dependent strong kin ties that remain in the country of origin. This would, in turn, reduce and eventually eliminate the level of remittances sent by migrant households.

HYPOTHESES AND MODEL

Remittance theory attributes the decay in remittances through time to the decline in the level of altruism that migrants have for their families back home. As the migrants' commitment to their area of origin weakens, the frequency and amount of remittances will decline through time. However, as discussed in the first half of this chapter, there is little empirical support for the remittance decay hypothesis. Most research on remittance behavior has failed to find a negative association between time and remittances. In fact, some research, especially research on Pacific Island migrant populations, suggest that the probability of remitting and the amount remitted actually continue at high levels for long periods of time. This raises the question: Through time, does the frequency and amount of remittances decay, as suggested by the remittance decay hypothesis, or continue, as suggested by empirical research?

Rather than viewing remittance decay as the result of migrants' declining altruism and commitment, the sociological approach to remittance behavior, as outlined in the second half of this chapter, views remittance decay – or duration – as a reflection of the state of the relationship between migrants and non-migrants. Remittances are the resources exchanged by members of a social network and exist because migrants are working to maintain their social capital. In the economic approach to remittances, it is generally assumed that remittances occur because the migrant is motivated by feelings of altruism, self-interest, fear of risk, etc. In the sociological approach, while migrants are motivated to remit by different types of social capital, including value introjection, reciprocity exchanges, and enforceable trust, their motivation is a by-product of the relationship previously established with a non-migrant. In other words, remittances occur because the migrant has established and is maintaining a relationship with another member of a social network. Thus, the reason for and the continuing existence of that relationship are more important for explaining remittance behavior, including both decay and duration, than is the motivation for remitting itself.

Why do remittances continue through time? Research has demonstrated that remittances are most often exchanged between immediate kin, including parents, spouses, children, and siblings. This is because strong kin ties are the most likely of all network ties to survive the migration process. They are also the most likely of all ties in which financial aid, including remittances, is exchanged. Thus, strong kin ties form the basis of remittance behavior. The migration process separates those strong kin ties in space and time. Remittances will persist as long as those strong kin ties between migrants and non-migrants continue to exist, are not dissolved through migration or death, and maintain a social support function that includes the exchange of financial aid, such as remittances.

While the strong ties between migrants and non-migrants form the basis of remittance behavior, the type of migration that establishes the household overseas can influence whether or not remittances occur and whether they decay through time. With family migration, the majority – if not all – of a household's strong kin ties migrate together overseas. Because few – if any – immediate kin are left behind in the country of origin, remittances are not likely to be sent overseas. With family chain migration, the strong kin ties of a household migrate over a period of time, splitting the household between country of origin and country of destination. Because of this split, household remittance behavior will be shaped by the family chain migration process. The goal of family chain migration is the reunification of the household overseas. As the family resettles in the country of destination, remittance levels will increase and may even achieve a constant level through time, but as fewer and fewer immediate kin remain in the country of destination, remittances will begin to decline. As this reunification process is completed, and the last dependent non-migrant joins the household overseas, the level of remittances will decline and end.

Not all immediate kin will join the migrant household overseas. In this case, as long as the strong kin ties are not dissolved by death and maintain a social support function that includes the exchange of financial aid, remittances sent to those non-migrant relatives will persist through time. Migrant network participation, by slowing the rate of adaptation and assimilation to the destination country and maximizing links with the origin society, will encourage both migrants and non-migrants to maintain their relationships through time. By helping to maintain these relationships, network participation should encourage sustained remittance behavior as well. The cultural orientation engendered by migrant network participation should also have a positive influence on remittance behavior. Because migrant networks link migrants to their origin cultures, the same social sanctions that discourage reneging on commitments back home will have been transplanted overseas. This will encourage migrants who are active network members to maintain their relationships overseas and continue remitting.

Guided by both the theoretical and empirical literature reviewed in this chapter, the following hypotheses are derived:

Hypothesis 1: When remittance behavior is modeled at the household level, remittances will exhibit a pattern of decay.

Hypothesis 2: Households that are reconstituted overseas through a process of family chain migration are more likely to remit than households whose members migrated at the same time.

Hypothesis 3: Households whose members participate in migrant networks are more likely to remit than are households whose members have isolated themselves from migrant networks.

The hypotheses and their related sub-hypotheses will be discussed in greater detail in the analytical chapters (chapters five through seven).

A Conceptual Model of Household Remittance Behavior

The conceptual model of household level remittance behavior used in this research is diagrammed in figure 2-2. At any point in time, the amount of remittances sent overseas by a migrant household is determined by both the household's probability of remitting and the financial ability to do so. Only the economic ability to remit directly influences the amount remitted. All other influences work indirectly through the probability of remitting. The probability of remitting is 1) directly influenced by the economic ability to remit, 2) directly influenced by household network participation, 3) directly influenced

Figure 2-2:   Model of Household Remittance Behavior

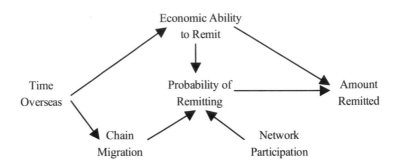

by chain migration into the household, and 4) indirectly influenced by the passage of time through the economic ability to remit and the level of chain migration. The economic ability to remit, migrant network participation, and level of chain migration should all be positively associated with the probability of remitting. As the household's financial resources increase, the household's probability of remitting should increase, which will indirectly increase the amount remitted. Active network participation should also increase the household's probability of remitting and indirectly the amount remitted. As an indicator of family chain migration, the occurrence of chain migration should increase the household's probability of remitting and the amount remitted as well

The number of years the household has been overseas indirectly influences both the probability of remitting and the amount remitted by influencing the economic ability to remit. For example, through time, members of a migrant household may obtain job skills that result in higher income, increasing the probability that more remittances will be sent home. The number of years spent overseas also indirectly influences the probability of remitting and the amount remitted by influencing chain migration. Because family reunification migration occurs over a period of time, the number of years the household has been established overseas can influence the level of chain migration experienced by the household. This can have both a positive and negative influence on the probability of remitting. Households that have experienced a low level of chain migration may be in the early stages of the reunification process when the majority of strong ties are in the country of origin and the probability of remitting, and indirectly the amount remitted, is high. Conversely, households that have experienced a high level of chain migration may be in the later stages of the reunification process when the probability of remitting, and the amount remitted, is declining and ending.

This chapter has described the results of the theoretical and empirical studies used to develop the sociological framework used in this research. The next chapter describes the data and methodology used in the analyses. Chapter four provides a brief history of the Micronesian migrant communities in Hawaii and Guam and a description of the characteristics of the migration flows. The establishment histories and characteristics of the communities are significant because they help explain the differences that exist between the Guam and Hawaii statistical models. Chapters five through seven present the results of the analyses.

CHAPTER 3
Modeling Household Remittance Behavior

THE CENSUS OF MICRONESIAN MIGRANTS

This study is based on data derived from the Census of Micronesian Migrants to Hawaii, Guam, and the Commonwealth of Northern Marianas (CNMI). The Census of Micronesian Migrants was funded by the US Department of the Interior's Office of Insular Affairs and collected and processed by the US Census Bureau's International Programs Center in 1997 and 1998. The purpose of the survey was to provide data to assess the impact of the Compact of Free Association, which allows citizens of the Federated States of Micronesia (FSM), the Republic of Marshall Islands (RMI), and the Republic of Palau to migrate freely to the United States and its territories and commonwealths.[iii] The surveys in Hawaii and Guam were fielded in 1997, while the survey in the CNMI was conducted in both 1997 and 1998. Only the information about Micronesians on Hawaii and Guam is released as public use data. As can be seen in table 3-1, the Micronesian migration flows to both Hawaii and Guam have been dominated by migrants from the FSM, as indicated by the proportion of FSM migrant households.[iv] Because of this dominance, the analyses focus solely on the remittance behavior of households with migrants from the FSM, an island nation in the north Pacific.

Table 3-1:   Proportion of Households with Migrants from the Federated States of Micronesia, Palau, and the Marshall Islands, Guam and Hawaii, 1997

Country of Origin	Country or State of Destination		
	Guam	Hawaii	Total
FSM	76.29	59.92	67.07
Palau	22.02	9.68	15.06
Marshall Islands	1.69	30.40	17.87
Total Number of Households	1,477	1,829	3,246

Advantages of the Data Set

The information provided by the Census of Micronesian Migrants to Guam and Hawaii is advantageous for studying the influence of family chain migration and network participation on remittance behavior for five reasons. First, it has information about the amount of remittances sent overseas by all households. Unlike other data sets, it also includes the amount of remittances received by the migrants from their families overseas. Second, the data set consists entirely of migrant households. In many data sets (e.g., SIPP and CPS data sets), migrant households make up only a small part of the total data set. This means that the sample size of migrant households in the Micronesian Census is large when compared to the data sets used by other researchers, which are often restricted to a few hundred households only. Third, it contains demographic information on all individuals in the household, including migration information, such as migration status and time of arrival. This information is essential for calculating variables, such as the number of migrants in the household or the years since the arrival of the earliest migrant, that were not included in the data set and that are essential for the analysis. Fourth, it also contains a wide range of household demographic, income, and expenditure data. Finally, although the design is not longitudinal, it contains sufficient retrospective information to estimate models of remittance behavior based on duration. Also, the duration variable is of sufficient depth. For example, the data includes information on FSM migrants who have been resident in Guam or Hawaii for well over 15 years.

Sampling, Data Collection, and Quality Control[v]

Although the Micronesian Census is referred to as a census, it is actually a survey of Micronesian migrants in Hawaii, Guam, and the CNMI. Micronesian migrants were defined as persons born in the FSM, Palau, or the Marshall Islands, or a child of someone born in one of those places. When a Micronesian household was identified, all individuals in the household were enumerated, even those not defined as Micronesian.

Each enumerator in Guam, Hawaii, and the CNMI was assigned an "enumeration district" based on geographic districts of *the countries of origin*. These districts were usually all or part of Palau and the Marshall Islands or a state within the FSM. For example, an enumerator would be responsible for canvassing a particular group, such as all migrants from the Micronesian state of Chuuk residing in Hawaii. If language or cultural barriers existed, the FSM states were further divided into smaller districts. The FSM states were also further divided if their overseas communities were too large for a single enumerator to efficiently canvass.

The Micronesian Census was collected using the "snowball" sampling technique. Migrants from Palau, the Marshall Islands, and the FSM living in Guam, Hawaii, or the CNMI were hired as enumerators and were responsible for enumerating the migrant households from their country/state of origin. The enumerators generated an initial list of Micronesian households based on personal acquaintances. Enumerators visited each household and conducted a personal interview, asking the questions worded on the Census questionnaire and recording the answers. At the end of each interview, the respondents were asked for the names of other migrants from their island. These names were added to the original list and the additional households were enumerated, again asking for the name and address of other migrants from their island. This process continued until no new names/households were added to the list.

The questionnaires use standard census data questions and include both basic and detailed population, housing, and expenditure questions. A single questionnaire contained all questions asked of every person in each housing unit. The questionnaires were originally identical for Guam, Hawaii, and the CNMI, but were modified at the request of each area to obtain data deemed particularly useful. For example, in Hawaii additional information on education and health was collected while in Guam additional housing information was obtained. The enumerator designated one person in each household as the "householder," or the main respondent. In most cases, the householder was the person, or one of the persons, who owned or rented the residence. If no such person existed, the enumerator or the members of the household would designate an adult household member age 15 years or older as the householder.

The Micronesian Census was executed by offices based locally in Guam, Hawaii, and the CNMI and was assisted by a coordinating staff that reported directly to the US Census Bureau. This organizational structure improved the quality of the data collected. Enumerators reviewed and edited questionnaires during field data collection operations for consistency, completeness, and acceptability. Local census office staff, assisted by the coordinating staff, also reviewed the questionnaires for omissions and inconsistencies. As a result of this review operation, enumerators made a telephone or a personal follow-up visit to obtain the missing information and a completed questionnaire. The local census staff, again assisted by the coordinating staff, keyed in the questionnaire data and completed initial computer edits that improved the quality and consistency of the data. The final data set was processed at the US Census Bureau in Washington, DC.

Duplicates in the Micronesian Census Data

The Micronesian Census includes 1,081 Micronesian households in Guam and 1,096 Micronesian households in Hawaii. However, a routine pre-analysis evaluation of the frequency distributions of the explanatory variables indicated the possibility of duplicates in the Hawaii data. Both the Guam and Hawaii data were visually examined to ensure that individuals within households were not reporting the same amount of remittances received or were not assigned the value reported by the householder. I created a table that listed all individuals who received remittances and the amount received by their household identification numbers. In the Guam data, thirty-one individuals received remittances, with only one household listing the same amount of remittances for all receiving members. In the Hawaii data, 193 individuals received remittances, with six households reporting the same amount of remittances received by their members. I concluded that the repeat reporting of remittances was not a systematic problem.

However, further examination of the table demonstrated the existence of duplicates in the Hawaii data. While the repeat reporting of remittances within households was not a problem, a pattern of repeat reporting between households was evident. Specifically, there were pairs of households that had the same number of individuals with the same person numbers receiving the same amount of remittances. A second table was created that listed non-remittance receiving households by their identification numbers, number of persons, and household income. Again, there were pairs of households that had the same number of persons and the same household income. A similar pattern was not found in the Guam data.

In order to purge the data of these duplicates in the Hawaii data, I wrote a SAS program that defined and removed duplicate households. Initially, I assumed that the duplicates were the result of clerical errors, for example, inputting the information from the same interview into the data set twice. If the duplicates were simply the result of input errors, any number of household-level variables should produce the same or a very similar number of duplicates. However, I found that different combinations of variables used to define duplicates resulted in a different number of duplicates. I then assumed that the duplicates were the result of enumerator deceit. Closer inspection of the data indicates this is probably true. I generated a table that listed households by their identification numbers and the values of 15 additional variables.[vi] Most of the suspected duplicates were identical on all of these variables except either the monthly electric or water bill. When comparing the duplicate pairs, the value of either the electric or water bill would usually differ between one and fifteen dollars, but sometimes the difference would be as high as one hundred dollars. Because of this pattern in the data, I assumed that one or more enumerators would complete a single interview and then fill out a second form, altering the values of a few variables, and submitting both forms to receive double pay.

To purge the duplicates from the data set, I defined a duplicate as any two households with the same value on the following household-level variables: 1) state and island of origin in FSM, 2) zip code in the state of Hawaii, 3) the total number of persons within the household, 4) household income, 5) monthly household rent, 6) the total amount of remittances received by individuals within a household, and 7) the amount of remittances sent by households overseas. I chose these variables for three reasons. First, when combined, these variables specifically define a household and reduce the likelihood that non-duplicate households would be defined as duplicates. Second, unlike the monthly electric and water bills, the values of these variables did not differ between duplicate pairs. Finally, except for two variables – the amount of remittances sent overseas and the total amount of remittances received by all individuals in the household – almost all households had a value for the remaining five variables.

Using the SAS program, I removed 290 FSM households (26 percent) from the Hawaii data set, reducing the sample size from 1,096 to 828. I tried different combinations of variables and the data were visually inspected after each run but, when compared to the seven variables I used in the SAS program, they either failed to remove the duplicates or removed cases that were not duplicates (e.g., when too few variables were used). While there is no guarantee that the SAS program removed all of the duplicates, it appears to have removed the majority of them. In a visual inspection of a sample of one hundred households, there were twenty-one duplicates and the SAS program removed just over 90 percent them.

The remaining duplicates should not negatively impact the analysis of remittance behavior in Hawaii. There are two reasons for this. First, there is no reason to believe that the duplicates in the data set are correlated to any one particular variable. Thus, the duplicates do not represent a systematic bias present in the data. Second, the presence of duplicates in the data does not appear to significantly inflate the standard errors in the regression analyses. I ran a test regression equation on the data set before and after the duplicates were removed. With the duplicates removed, the standard errors of the coefficients (not including the intercept) increased from between 2 percent to 18 percent, with an average of 11 percent. However, the pattern of significance among the variables did not change, even though the level of significance of a few of the variables declined slightly. Even if the remaining duplicates were removed, and assuming my estimate of approximately 10 percent remaining in the data set is correct, it is unlikely there removal would significantly further increase the value of the standard errors or change the significance pattern. Thus, with 90 percent of the duplicates removed, the conclusions derived from the significance tests associated with the regression analyses should be the same as if there were no duplicates at all. However, variables with "border-line" significance will be interpreted with caution.

Final Sample Size

The data samples used in this research consist of households where the earliest migrant was born in the Federated States of Micronesia and who live in either Guam or Hawaii. Households defined as Micronesian because a household member is a child of a Micronesian migrant were not included in the sample.[vii] The final sample has 1,078 FSM households in Guam and 791 FSM households in Hawaii.[viii] This includes 7,018 household members in Guam and 2,867 household members in Hawaii.

THE DEPENDENT VARIABLES

This research will focus on two related dependent variables: 1) whether or not the migrant household remitted money overseas and 2) the amount of money sent by remitting households. Both of these variables are derived from the question: "How much did all members of this household spend in the last twelve months on remittances overseas?" While the household probability of remitting was about the same for both Guam and Hawaii, Hawaii migrant households remitted at higher levels than did Guam households. Of the 1,078 FSM households in Guam, 404 households (37 percent) remitted money overseas in 1996, while among the 789 FSM households in Hawaii, 303 (38 percent) remitted. The FSM households in Guam sent an average of $177 per year, while the households in Hawaii averaged $285. Among remitting households, Guam households sent an average of $473, while Hawaii sent an average of $743.

Figure 3-1 shows the frequency distribution of the amount of money remitted in 1996 by FSM households in Guam and Hawaii. The higher average remittances sent by Hawaii households are reflected in the frequency distribution. Guam households were more likely than Hawaii households to send small amounts (less than $500 per year) while Hawaii households were more likely to send larger amount (more than $1,000 per year). Approximately 70 percent of the Guam remitting households sent less than $500, while over half (52 percent) of Hawaii remitting households sent over $500. Approximately 11 percent of Hawaii households remitted over $1,000, while only 6 percent of the Guam households did so. Regardless of these differences, the modal remitting category for both groups is less than $250.

Figure 3-1:   **Frequency Distribution of Amount of Money Remitted in 1996 by FSM Households, Guam and Hawaii, 1997**

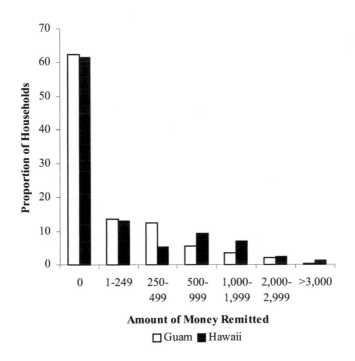

Amount of Money Remitted

☐ Guam ■ Hawaii

Time Profile of Remittances

The remittance duration variable used in this research is based on the number of years the earliest migrant in the household has been overseas. The information about the time of arrival of the earliest migrant is derived from the question: "In what month/year did ___ come to Hawaii/Guam to stay?" Using the number of years the earliest migrant has been overseas is a significant change from the way duration is measured in other remittance studies. Usually, duration is derived from the number of years the householder has been overseas. However, using the time overseas of the earliest migrant has two distinct advantages – it can be used as a household-level variable and is a better representation of household-level duration. Because the householder may or may not be the earliest migrant in the household, the time the householder has been overseas only measures the length of time that particular individual has been overseas and thus can only be used as an individual-level variable. However, the arrival time of the earliest migrant measures the maximum length of time that a migrant household has been established overseas. In this sense, the time overseas of the earliest migrant is a better representation of "household time." The advantages of using the time overseas of the earliest migrant as opposed to the time overseas of the householder is discussed more fully in chapter five.

To provide an initial indication of the relationship between household remittance behavior and time, I divided the time overseas by the earliest migrant into six three-year periods and estimated 1) the average total remittances per household, 2) the proportion of remitting households, and 3) the average total remittances per remitting household through time.[ix] These data, which are summarized in table 3-2, suggest that for both the Guam and Hawaii migrant communities there is some evidence of remittance decay, especially after approximately twelve years overseas. The average total remittances per household, the proportion of remitting households, and the average total remittances per remitting households are shown graphically in figures 3-2, 3-3 and 3-4.

The average remitted per household in both Guam and Hawaii shows a pattern of increase and decline through time. For both Guam and Hawaii, the per household remittance average (figure 3-2) increases during the first six years overseas, from $160 to $200 in Hawaii and from $75 to $175 in Guam. The average in Hawaii continues to increase, peaking at between nine and eleven years just over $400 per household, when it begins to decline to about $200 per household by years fifteen and over. The average remitted by Guam households remains fairly constant between six and fifteen years, increasing slightly to approximately $200. For both Guam and Hawaii,

Table 3-2:   Remittances by Time Overseas of the Earliest Migrant,
             Guam and Hawaii, 1997

Time Overseas, Earliest Migrant	Number of Households	Average, All Households	Proportion of Remitting Households	Average, Remitting Households
Guam				
0-2	86	77.44	27.91	277.50
3-5	199	175.26	37.69	465.03
6-8	442	179.70	34.62	519.14
9-11	222	206.49	44.14	467.76
12-14	71	213.03	43.66	487.90
15 and over	58	156.48	39.66	394.61
Total	1,078	177.19	37.48	472.79
Hawaii				
0-2	205	158.96	26.83	592.49
3-5	205	211.07	34.15	618.14
6-8	203	323.47	45.81	706.06
9-11	71	408.50	51.43	794.31
12-14	48	398.54	50.00	797.08
15 and over	57	214.29	41.07	521.74
Total	789	255.71	38.40	668.59

Note: The Hawaii sample contains two households that reported remitting $12,000 overseas. Because these values were unusually large and have such a large influence on the distribution of the data, they were excluded from the above table (but were included in all later statistical analyses). If they were included, the values for the 9-11 category would be $571.76 for the total household average, 52.11 for the proportion remitting, and $1,097.16 for the remitters' average. The values for the 15 and over category would be $421.05 for the total household average, 42.11 for the proportion remitting, and $1,000.00 for the remitters' average.

the average remitted by households overseas for more than fifteen years declines when compared to the twelve to fourteen year average, but remains higher than the average remitted during the first six years overseas.

The proportion of households remitting also shows this pattern of increase and decline. For the first six years, the proportion of Guam and Hawaii households remitting (figure 3-3) increases from approximately

Figure 3-2:   Average Remittances, All FSM Households, Guam and Hawaii, 1997

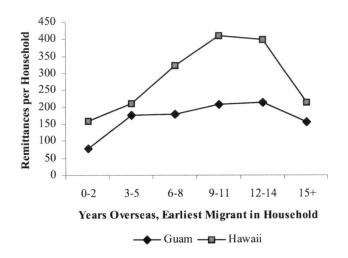

Figure 3-3:   Proportion of FSM Households Remitting, Guam and Hawaii, 1997

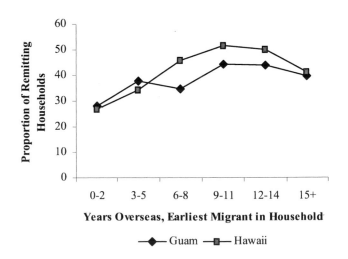

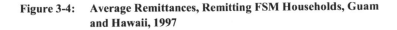

Figure 3-4:   Average Remittances, Remitting FSM Households, Guam and Hawaii, 1997

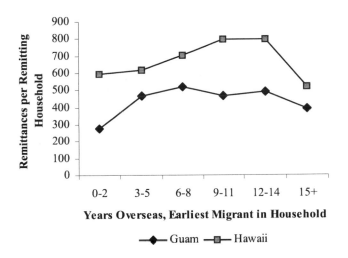

25 percent to 35 percent. Only the Hawaii households' probability of remitting continues to steadily increase until years nine to eleven, peaking at just over 50 percent. Between years twelve to fourteen and years fifteen and over, the probability for Hawaii households declines to about 40 percent, but remains higher than the probability of remitting for the first six years. For Guam, the probability of remitting also increases, but less steadily. The Guam household probability of remitting also peaks at years nine to eleven at approximately 45 percent, declining to about 40 percent by years fifteen and over. Again, for both Guam and Hawaii, the proportion of remitting households in the over fifteen years category remains higher than the proportion remitting in the first six years.

The pattern of increase and decline is less clear for the amount remitted by remitting households. For the Hawaii households, the amount remitted increases from just under $600 for years zero to two and increases steadily to just under $800 for years twelve to fourteen, declining to approximately $500 for years fifteen and over. For the Guam households, the amount remitted increases from approximately $275 for years zero to two but peaks at over $500 for years six to eight, a much earlier peak than the Hawaii households. After years six to eight, the amount remitted by the Guam households begins a slow decline to just under $400 for years fifteen and over.

The pattern of increase and decline in both the probability of remitting and the amount remitted lends support to the existence of remittance decay in these migrant communities. However, caution must be exercised in interpreting the descriptive analyses. Cross-tabulation analyses cannot control for other characteristics that could be important determinants of remittances and that could increase (or decrease) the strength of the association between remittance behavior and time. In this research, multivariate statistical techniques are used to assess the significance of duration while simultaneously controlling for other potential determinants of remittances. Details regarding my analytical methods and model are discussed in the next two sections and the results of the multivariate analyses are presented in chapters five through seven.

ANALYTICAL METHODS

Banerjee (1984) emphasizes that the choice of the appropriate regression model for the analysis of remittance data depends on whether the decision to remit and the amount remitted is seen as a one stage, simultaneous process or as a two stage, sequential process. Brown (1997, 1998) assumes that there is only one remittance decision in which the decision to remit and the amount remitted occurs simultaneously. He also assumes that the explanatory variables included in the model have an equal effect on the probability that the migrant is a remitter and on the level of remittances. Brown uses tobit regression and maximum likelihood analysis to model a single equation using data on both remitting and non-remitting migrants. Banerjee (1984), Hoddinott (1992), and Menjivar et al. (1998) assume the remittance decision is a two-stage process. They first model the discrete decision to remit using either a probit or logit model and then model the amount remitted using OLS regression. The advantage of this method is that the model can include two sets of variables, each influencing the different stages of the remittance process. There can even be variables that influence one part of the decision but not the other.

Hoddinott (1992) notes that migrant remittance theory, as defined by the writings of Stark and his colleagues, makes no distinction between factors influencing the likelihood that an individual will remit and the level of remittances. However, a number of authors have found that single variables will have varying effects on the likelihood of remitting, the amount remitted, and the economic ability to do so (Banerjee 1984; Funkhouser 1995; Massey and Basem 1992; Menjivar et al. 1998). Also, the sociological approach to remittance behavior, as interpreted and modeled in chapter two, makes an explicit distinction between the two stages (see figure 2-2). Thus, based on theory and the results of empirical studies, this research will model the remittance decision as a two-stage, sequential process with each stage influenced by a different but overlapping set of explanatory variables.

Logit/OLS v. Tobit

To account for the two-stage remittance decision process, I use separate equations explaining the households' likelihood (log odds) of remitting and, if remittances were sent, the amount remitted. I analyze the likelihood of remitting for the entire sample using logistic regression. For the sub-sample of those households that remit, I estimate an equation explaining the natural logarithm of the amount remitted by OLS regression. I use the natural logarithm of the amount remitted to compress the wide range of this variable and to adjust for its skewness.

A number of researchers prefer to use tobit regression when analyzing remittance data (e.g., *see* Brown 1997). However, tobit regression is a more restrictive model because it uses only one set of coefficients to simultaneously explain the likelihood to remit and the amount remitted. Because I am interested in separately analyzing the influence of variables on the likelihood of remitting and on the amount remitted, I use a combination of logistic and OLS regression in my analyses.

Logit/OLS and the Issue of Sample Selection

The sample of Micronesian migrant households can be divided into remitting and non-remitting households. While the entire sample can be used in the logistic regression analysis to determine the likelihood of remitting, only a portion of the sample (i.e., those that have remitted) can be used to estimate the association between household characteristics and the amount remitted. However, the sample of households that remit may be a selective sample of all those that have remitted. This raises the question of whether or not to correct the analyses for possible sample selection bias.

Many studies have chosen to ignore the problem of sample selection, paying no special attention to non-remitters (e.g., Johnson and Whitelaw 1974; Rempel and Lobdell 1978; Lucas and Stark 1985). However, including non-remitters in OLS regression analyses (i.e., as remitting zero dollars) with remitters can result in biased and inconsistent parameter estimates (Breen 1996; Brown 1997). Others have attempted to avoid this problem by restricting their samples to remitters only (e.g., Knowles and Anker 1981), but this has also been shown to result in biased and inconsistent estimates (Brown 1997). Most of the more recent remittance research using probit/logit and OLS test for problems of sample selection using the method described by Heckman (1979). Much of this research (Funkhouser 1995; Massey and Basem 1992; Menjivar et al. 1998) has failed to find significant selection effects.

Menjivar et al. (1998:111-112) note that, in remittance research, the challenge is trying to find a particular variable (or set of variables) that influences the probability of remitting but not the amount remitted. When analyzing sex-based earnings differentials, for example, it is standard practice in the economic literature to first control for the influence of the lower labor force participation rates of women due to marital status, number of children, education level, etc. Menjivar et al. (1998) found no such indicator in their data. In this research, the conceptual framework used and discussed in chapter two does not define any particular variable as a selection variable. Because much of the more recent research on remittance behavior has failed to find a sample selection effect, and because the conceptual framework used in this analysis failed to suggest one or more selection variables, I have decided not correct for sample selection bias.

One Sample or Two?

In order to determine if the Guam and Hawaii samples could be grouped into a single data set, I ran t-tests to test for the difference between the means of a variety of variables, including many of the explanatory variables used in the analyses. On almost all of the means tested, the Guam and Hawaii samples were significantly different. I concluded that the two samples were too statistically different to be combined into a single sample, so in this research the Guam and Hawaii samples are analyzed separately.

Statistical Program

I use the SAS statistical program, including the logistic and OLS regression packages, to complete all of the analyses in this research.

A HOUSEHOLD MODEL OF REMITTANCE BEHAVIOR

Most research in the remittance literature uses individual-level models to analyze remittance behavior. Some of this research (Funkhouser 1995; Hoddinott 1982; Johnson and Whitelaw 1974) uses both an individual-level dependent variable and an individual-level duration variable. For example, Johnson and Whitelaw (1974) use the proportion of monthly income remitted by the male migrant respondent to his rural household as the dependent variable and the years of urban residence by the migrant as the duration variable. Other researchers use a household-level dependent variable and an individual-level duration variable (Banerjee 1984; Brown 1998; Knowles and Anker 1981; Menjivar et al. 1998). For example, Brown (1998) uses the amount of money remitted by the household overseas as the dependent variable and the number of months since the migrant head of household emigrated as the duration variable. Regardless of the analytical level used for the dependent and duration variables, all studies of remittance behavior control for additional individual and household-level characteristics. However, regardless of this mix, the models used in the remittance literature remain fundamentally individual-level models because their goal is to explain individual, not household, behavior.

Usually, the analytical level of the dependent variable is determined by the questions used in the survey to gather remittance data (i.e., whether or not the survey asked every individual in the household how much they remitted or just asked for the household total). However, the questions asked – and to whom – can also determine the analytical level of the explanatory variables, including the duration variable (i.e., whether or not the survey gathered information about all members of the household or just the migrant householder), as noted by Menjivar et al. (1998:123). The Micronesian Census includes data only on the total amount of remittances sent overseas by the migrant households, not the amounts sent by the individual household members. Thus, both my dependent variables are household-level variables. Fortunately, the Micronesian Census collected household demographic, income, and expenditure data as well as information on all individuals in the household, including detailed demographic and migration history information. This allows me to control for household-level variables already available in the data set as well as create new household-level variables by summing the characteristics of the individual members (e.g., the number of migrants in the household, the proportion of female to male migrants, etc.). This flexibility has allowed me to model remittance behavior solely at the household level.

The choice of a household-level model is more than simply an effort to use variables at a single analytical level but an attempt to capture the behavior of households as social units. Remittance decisions are made by household members and made within the socio-economic context of those households. Thus, ascribing household-level behavior to the characteristics of a single household member is error prone. There are two reasons why this is so. First, using the characteristics of one household member, such as the householder or household head, assumes a single, primary decision-maker. However, there may be in fact more than one decision-maker (e.g., a migrant and a spouse) or the decision-making process was strongly influenced by multiple household members (e.g., all adult members, all migrants, etc.). Second, even if a primary decision-maker exists in a household, there is no guarantee that the individual chosen to represent the household will be the chief decision-maker. The characteristics incorporated into the analyses may or may not be those of the primary decision-maker. This is especially true in surveys where information is taken for only one respondent in each household and where the main respondent is chosen randomly (e.g., whoever "answers the door") rather than for specific reasons (e.g., the primary income earner). Also, assuming the existence of a chief decision-maker, large variations in household size can introduce non-systematic error. Obviously, in a household with one occupant, the primary decision-maker is that individual. For small households with, for example, two to three individuals, there is a high probability that the individual randomly chosen to represent the household is the primary decision-maker. However, in larger households with, for example, eight to ten individuals, that probability is significantly reduced. Thus, attributing the behavior of households to the characteristics of an individual member risks eliminating the contextual information so important to explaining group-decision making and behavior and, worse, may ultimately result in misleading conclusions.

Criticisms of Household-Based Models in Migration Research

Focusing on the household as the unit of analysis explicitly recognizes that migrants live with others in social contexts that influence their behavior. However, this approach has been criticized for effectively substituting a rational, calculating individual with a rational, calculating household (Folbre 1996; Gos and Lindquist 1995). Critics have objected to the view of the household as a "unified strategic actor" and the idea that migrant households are organized solely on principles of reciprocity, consensus, and altruism (Pessar 1999; Grieco and Boyd 1998). While the orientation and actions of household members can be guided by norms of solidarity, they can also be directed by hierarchies of power, especially those based on gender (Pessar 1999; Hondagneu-Sotelo 1992). Household decisions and actions do not represent unified and equally beneficial outcomes for all members (Boyd 1989a; Ellis, Conway and Bailey 1996; Gos and Lindquist 1996; Pedraza 1991). This is because households, as units where production and redistribution take place, represent centers of struggle where people with different activities and interests can come into conflict with one another (Hartmann 1981). Such diverse interests and activities, when situated within the ongoing power relations that operate in households, strongly suggest that the action and goals of male and female members do not always coincide and may not always create equal or beneficial outcomes (Curtis 1986; Hondagneu-Sotelo 1992, 1994; Grasmuck and Pessar 1991). Recognizing the influence of power hierarchies within households is therefore essential to fully understanding differences in the migration-related behavior of men and women.

The same criticism leveled at the use of a "unitary household model" (Hondagneu-Sotelo 1992) in the study of migration could, of course, be directed at its use in remittance research. It stands to reason that the hierarchies of power in a household that differentially influence the migration decision-making abilities of men and women would also differentially influence their remittance behavior. In this study, I focus on explaining the decay of remittances at the household level through time and not on gendered behavioral differences. However, the sociological approach used to guide this research could easily be extended to explain the existence of differential remittance behavior of men and women, as I discuss more fully in chapter seven. Unfortunately, the Micronesian Census presents limits to a more gendered analysis. Specifically, it only includes data on the aggregate amount of remittances sent by the migrant households, not the amounts sent by the individual household members. A gendered analysis of household remittance behavior would require knowing both the amount of remittances sent by and the sex of each member of the household.

The Explanatory Variables

The explanatory variables included in the logistic and OLS statistical models will include measures of the length of time the household has been overseas, the household's economic ability to remit, the process of chain migration, and indirect measures of the household's network participation. Table 3-3 lists the explanatory variables used in the statistical models discussed in chapters five through seven and provides descriptive statistics for both the Guam and Hawaii samples. Table 3-4 shows the means of the descriptive statistics for remitting households only. The meaning and theoretical significance of the individual variables will be discussed in greater detail in the analytical chapters.

This chapter has described the data and the methodology used in this analysis. The next chapter briefly reviews the history of the Federated States of Micronesia, placing emphasis on the social, economic, and political trends that lead to the establishment of the Micronesian migrant communities in Guam and Hawaii. In the second half of chapter four, several characteristics that demonstrate important differences between the migrant communities are described and compared. In summary, the descriptive data suggests that, when compared to Hawaii, the migration flow to Guam is older and dominated by family reunification migration to older, well-established homes. Hawaii has a higher proportion of single-migrant households, newly arrived migrants, and newly established households that also indicate the flow to Hawaii is younger than that to Guam. The comparative age of the flows is significant to this study because it helps explain some of the differences found in the Guam and Hawaii statistical analyses presented in chapters five through seven.

Table 3-3: **Descriptive Statistics for the Explanatory Variables Used in the Analytical Models, All Households, Guam and Hawaii, 1997**

Category/Variable	Guam (N=1,078)		Hawaii (N=791)	
	Mean	SD	Mean	SD
Remittance Duration				
Years Overseas, Earliest Migrant	7.67	4.00	6.24	5.36
Years Since Arrival of Last Migrant	2.98	3.02	2.93	3.99
Household Financial Resources				
Adult Equivalent Income (per $1,000)	6.44	7.65	9.03	21.97
Number of Migrants Age 16 and Over	3.94	2.37	2.41	1.64
Proportion of Migrants Age 16 and Over in the Labor Force	58.67	35.49	54.21	41.76
Continued Migration				
Number of Migrant Groups That Arrived between the Earliest and Latest Migrants	1.04	1.30	0.55	0.91
Family Reunification: (a)				
Earliest Migrant and All Relatives in the Household Migrated in the Same Year	0.14		0.09	
Earliest Migrant and One or More Relatives in Household Migrated in Different Years	0.80		0.48	
Single Migrant in Household, Alone or with Non-Relatives	0.06		0.43	
Network Participation				
Social Expenditures as a Percent of Total Household Income	0.10	0.43	0.06	0.33
Percent of Non-Micronesians in Household	0.02	0.10	0.07	0.20
Trips to the FSM (a)	0.50		0.17	
Receipt of Remittances by Household from Overseas(a)	0.02		0.13	
English Use in the Home:(a)				
Other Exclusively or Other More Frequently Than English	0.76		0.51	
Other and English Equally or Other Less Frequently Than English	0.07		0.23	
English Exclusively	0.17		0.26	

Note: Each mean is based on a sub-sample of cases without missing values.
(a): Dummy variable(s)

Table 3-4:   **Descriptive Statistics for the Explanatory Variables Used in the Analytical Models, Remitting Households Only, Guam and Hawaii, 1997**

Category/Variable	Guam (N=404)		Hawaii (N=303)	
	Mean	SD	Mean	SD
Remittance Duration				
Years Overseas, Earliest Migrant	7.97	3.77	6.88	4.68
Years Since Arrival of Last Migrant	2.67	2.69	2.98	3.65
Household Financial Resources				
Adult Equivalent Income (per $1,000)	8.21	6.95	12.18	12.72
Number of Migrants Age 16 and Over	4.46	2.57	2.71	1.69
Proportion of Migrants Age 16 and Over in the Labor Force	69.45	28.32	72.86	31.12
Continued Migration				
Number of Migrant Groups That Arrived between the Earliest and Latest Migrants	1.33	1.43	0.69	0.98
Family Reunification: (a)				
Earliest Migrant and All Relatives in the Household Migrated in the Same Year	0.09		0.07	
Earliest Migrant and One or More Relatives in Household Migrated in Different Years	0.88		0.57	
Single Migrant in Household, Alone or with Non-Relatives	0.03		0.35	
Network Participation				
Social Expenditures as a Percent of Total Household Income	0.15	0.55	0.11	0.50
Percent of Non-Micronesians in Household	0.01	0.07	0.07	0.19
Trips to the FSM (a)	0.75		0.23	
Receipt of Remittances by Household from Overseas(a)	0.03		0.13	
English Use in the Home:(a)				
Other Exclusively or Other More Frequently Than English	0.88		0.62	
Other and English Equally or Other Less Frequently Than English	0.06		0.27	
English Exclusively	0.06		0.11	

Note: Each mean is based on a sub-sample of cases without missing values.
(a): Dummy variable(s)

CHAPTER 4

Migrants from the Federated States of Micronesia

This chapter presents a brief history of the Federated States of Micronesia (FSM) and the establishment of the Micronesian migrant communities in Guam and Hawaii. In order to understand the timing and reasons for Micronesian emigration to overseas destinations, it is first necessary to understand the history of the FSM, especially its colonial relationship with the United States. This is because the postwar policies of the United States government in the Pacific generated major changes that eventually lead to the massive surge of out-migration in the late 1980s. This chapter begins with a brief review of the post-1850 history of the FSM, placing emphasis on the post-1945 period of political and economic dominance by the United States in Micronesia. The discussion highlights those demographic and socio-economic trends that have significantly influenced the mobility, both internal and international, of the FSM people.

After explaining how and why Micronesians emigrated from the FSM, several social, economic, and migration characteristics of the Micronesian communities in both Guam and Hawaii are described and compared. Emphasis is placed on those characteristics that, as suggested by the migration history literature, may differentially influence household remittance behavior. This description has three objectives. First, it will show that the migration flow to Guam is older than the flow to Hawaii. Second, it will show that the older migration flow to Guam is dominated by family reunification migration, while the younger flow to Hawaii exhibits characteristics of an early labor migration flow. Finally, it will demonstrate that the households in Guam are larger and more established, financially and socially, than the households in Hawaii. These differences are significant because of the implications they may have for remittance behavior. Older, more financially stable migrant households reestablishing themselves overseas through a process of family chain migration may be both better able and more likely to remit than younger, financially unstable households at the beginning of the family reunification process. The implications of these differences are further discussed at the end of this chapter.

THE FEDERATED STATES OF MICRONESIA

The FSM is located approximately 2,500 miles south-west of Hawaii and consists of 607 islands spread through approximately one million square miles in the western Pacific Ocean. Although the area encompassing the FSM is large, the total land area is only 271 square miles. The 607 islands vary from large, mountainous islands of volcanic origin to small atolls (FSM National Census Office 1996). There are four states in the FSM: Yap, Chuuk, Pohnpei, and Kosrae. Yap, the westernmost state, consists of the Yap Islands, a group of four limestone high islands, and nine coral atolls and six smaller islands at varying distance from the high islands. The Yap Islands, which also contain the state capital of Colonia, dominate the politics and economy of the state. Chuuk, which is near the geographic center of the FSM, consists of Chuuk Lagoon, a complex of nineteen volcanic islands and twenty-four coral islands encircled by a barrier reef, and twelve coral atolls and outer islands. The islands of Chuuk Lagoon, which include the state capital of Moen (on Weno Island), dominate the state economically, politically, and demographically. Pohnpei, which is located in the eastern half of the FSM, consists of volcanic Pohnpei Island and eight coral atolls. Pohnpei Island, which includes the state and national capital of Kolonia, dominates the politics and economy of the state, and with over 90 percent of the state population living on the island, dominates the state demographically as well. Kosrae, the easternmost state in the FSM, is an archipelago consisting of fifteen islands within a fringing reef, although historically people have lived on only two islands, Ualang and Lelu. Ualang is the largest island in the archipelago while Lelu is a smaller island located in a bay about 1,600 feet from the northeastern coast of Ualang. Lelu Island dominates Kosrae economically, politically, and demographically, with Lelu Village being both the capital and largest community in the state (Gorenflo 1993,1995; Gorenflo and Levin 1991, 1992, 1995).

A BRIEF POST-CONTACT HISTORY OF THE FSM

During the early sixteenth century, Spanish explorers claimed the FSM[x] as part of Spain's growing Pacific Empire, but apart from brief visits by Europeans and Americans during the early nineteenth century, there was little contact between the island inhabitants and non-Micronesians until the mid-1800s. Spain exercised little authority over the area until the 1870s, when small settlements on Pohnpei and Yap Islands were established, partially in response to the growing economic competition in the area from other nations, especially Germany. Following Spain's defeat in the Spanish-American war, Germany purchased the FSM and other Pacific territories from Spain in 1899. Germany made the first serious attempt to colonize and develop the region. At the onset of Germany's involvement in World War I in 1914, Japanese military forces occupied German-held Micronesian territories. With their occupation sanctioned by the League of Nations in 1920, Japan continued to administer the area until 1945. The colonization and development efforts by Japan were much more intensive than that of either Spain or Germany, especially during the years prior to World War II (Gorenflo and Levin 1992, 1995).

The United States occupied the FSM following the Japanese surrender in 1945 and in 1947 the islands became part of the Trust Territory of the Pacific Islands (TTPI).[xi] The TTPI was a strategic area established by the United Nations and administered by the United States. Because its interests in the area were more strategic than economic, the United States began returning the responsibilities of government and business to the native people during the first decade of its administration. However, under successive administrations by the US Navy (1945-1951) and the US Department of the Interior (1952-1986), the United States economic involvement gradually intensified. In 1979, the former TTPI districts of Yap, Chuuk, Pohnpei, and Kosrae approved a constitution and became a self-governing nation, separate from the remaining TTPI areas. The US Government ratified the Compact of Free Association in 1986, officially ending its administration and defining future relations between the newly-independent FSM and the United States (Gorenflo 1993, 1995; Gorenflo and Levin 1992, 1993). Because of limited industry and development potential, it is likely that the FSM will have to depend on US aid to buttress its economy, so the United States will retain political and economic influence in the FSM for the indefinite future.

THE ESTABLISHMENT OF MIGRATION FLOWS FROM THE FSM TO GUAM AND HAWAII

A small number of Micronesians began migrating to other Pacific Islands as early as the 1960s, but emigration from the FSM to the United States and its territories and commonwealths, including Hawaii and Guam, began in earnest in the late 1980s after the signing of the Compact of Free Association. This surge in emigration can be attributed to a clause in the Compact that grants FSM citizens the right to enter, reside, and work anywhere in the United States, including its Pacific territories and commonwealths. While the Compact helps explain the timing of these migration flows, in order to understand how and why these flows were established, it is first necessary to understand the history of the FSM, especially its on-going historic relationship with the United States. This is because the social, political, and economic policies of the United States generated changes within the FSM that caused a dramatic increase in internal migration and, combined with Compact implementation, resulted in the massive surge of out-migration in the 1980s. This section reviews the US Pacific policies in the post-war period that helped establish the migration flows from the FSM to Guam and Hawaii. This overview highlights those historic trends that helped define many of the characteristics of the Guam and Hawaii migrant communities. These characteristics are important because they help explain the differences in the remittance behavior of the two communities.

Trends in Population Decline and Growth

Diseases introduced by Western explorers, whalers, missionaries, and other early visitors in the 1800s caused a period of sustained depopulation in the FSM. Infectious diseases such as smallpox, measles, and influenza caused sharp increases in mortality rates while venereal diseases simultaneously lowered fertility rates, leading to population decline. The rate of decline varied among the states of the FSM. For example, the island groups in Chuuk had relatively little sustained contact with the west until the late nineteenth century, which reduced the relative amount of depopulation that occurred. However, in Kosrae state, depopulation was particularly rapid and severe, nearly eradicating the native inhabitants between 1830 and 1880 (Gorenflo 1995; Gorenflo and Levin 1992, 1995). The timing of population recovery also varied among the states. Population growth began in Kosrae in the late 1800s and, between 1920 and 1950, the populations of Kosrae and Pohnpei continued to increase. The population of Chuuk state remained relatively constant during the Japanese administration, while the population of Yap state continued to decline until the early to mid-1950s. At least part of the population recovery during the first half of the nineteenth century was due to the efforts by the Japanese administration to control infectious diseases through public health measures (Gorenflo 1993, 1995; Gorenflo and Levin 1991, 1992).

During the United States administration of the TTPI, the population of the FSM grew rapidly. This is attributed to the introduction and widespread availability of modern medicine and health technology in the immediate post-war period, which helped control many of the diseases that persisted until the end of World War II. After the mid-1950s, the populations of each state experienced sustained and often rapid growth, resulting in modern populations larger than those previously recorded (Gorenflo 1993, 1995; Gorenflo and Levin 1991, 1992). This rapid growth continued into the 1980s and is reflected in the high annual inter-censal growth rates of 2.3 percent for 1973 to 1980 and 3.0 percent for 1980 to 1989. The annual growth rates reported by all the states were uniformly high for much of the 1980s, ranging from 2.7 percent for Chuuk (1980 to 1989) to 4.6 percent for Pohnpei (1980 to 1985). The rapid population growth of the 1950s through the 1970s began to slow down in the early-to-mid 1980s. All the states showed a significant decline in their annual growth rates between the mid-to-late 1980s and 1994. The rates ranged from between 1.3 percent for Kosrae (1986 to 1994) to 2.2 percent for Chuuk (1990 to 1994). For all of the FSM, the annual growth rate between 1989 and 1994 declined to 1.9 percent (FSM National Census Office 1996). While the population of the FSM has continued to grow, the decline in the annual growth rate for this period can be partially attributed to the increase in emigration. As of 1994, the population of the FSM was 105,506 – 50.5 percent in Chuuk, 31.9 percent in Pohnpei, 10.6 percent in Yap and 6.9 percent in Kosrae (FSM National Census Office 1996).

Post-War Economic Development in the TTPI

During the first fifteen years of its administration, the United States made little effort to develop Micronesia economically or move its people towards an independent political status. At this time, many of the Trust Territory citizens reverted to subsistence agriculture and a way of life typical of the period preceding the Japanese administration (Peoples 1986; Gorenflo and Levin 1995). In the early 1960s, a critical report issued by a United Nations Visiting Mission galvanized the United States into taking a more active role in the economic development of the TTPI. In 1963, funds appropriated by the US Congress to be spent on Micronesia more than doubled to $15 million. The funding continued to increase to $48 million in 1970 and $90 million in 1977, peaking at $138 million in 1979 (Hezel and McGrath

1989; Peoples 1986). This infusion of funds increased employment opportunities and moved the FSM from a subsistence agricultural economy to a wage labor economy (Gorenflo 1993; Peoples 1986). It also improved the material living standards of Micronesia. Most were spent on the improvement of social services (primarily education and health), government administration, economic and political development, and capital improvement projects, such as school buildings, roads, and airports (Peoples 1986). As a result, the majority of the work force was employed by either the federal or state governments, with most of the private businesses ultimately relying on these funds as well (Gorenflo 1993; Hezel and McGrath 1989; Peoples 1986). The FSM economy continued to be dominated by the public sector through the 1980s and 1990s. The 1980 and 1994 FSM censuses reported that approximately 42 percent of employed persons were in either the public administration or education industries (FSM National Census Office 1996).

The development of a wage labor economy in the 1960s caused an increase in internal migration in the FSM. While the early years of the United States administration of the TTPI was a period of limited mobility, increasing economic opportunities, especially in the emerging population centers within each state, resulted in an increase in rural to urban and outer island to main island migration (Gorenflo and Levin 1995). In the 1970s, the places with the largest immigrant populations tended to be those that were experiencing rapid development and offered modern amenities such as wage employment, advanced education, and Western medical treatment (Gorenflo and Levin 1995). In-migration to the urban centers was at its height in the 1970s (Hezel and Levin 1990) and the concentration of the population on certain island groups or in certain municipalities was quite dramatic. In 1973, over 75 percent of the population of Chuuk lived on Chuuk Lagoon, with over one-fourth living on Weno Island. Over 65 percent of the total population of Yap state lived on Yap Proper, with approximately 32 percent of the total state population living on the islands of Rull and Weloy. On Pohnpei, approximately 90 percent of the states' population lived in the Central Municipalities, with over one-fourth living in the capital of Kolonia. In Kosrae, over one-third of its total population lived on the island of Lelu (Gorenflo 1993, 1995; Gorenflo and Levin 1991, 1992).

The Micronesian "Education Explosion"

Much of the internal migration in each state was the result of students moving to central urban areas for education. This migration was the result of the United States education policy in Micronesia. The policy of universal education through high school in the United States Pacific and the infusion of funds into the TTPI beginning in the 1960s resulted in a rapid growth of the education industry and a dramatic increase in the number of high school graduates. The growth of the education sector throughout Micronesia began in the 1960s with the construction of new elementary and secondary schools, the recruitment of new teachers from the United States, and the commitment of a much larger share of the Trust Territory's growing budget to education (Barringer, Gardner, and Levin 1993; Hezel and Levin 1990). By the mid-1960s, the four states in the FSM had their own public high schools and some had private high schools as well. By the end of the decade, high school enrollments had soared and continued to increase into the 1970s. The increases were often quite dramatic, as noted by Hezel (1978:26) for Chuuk: "The total population of (Chuuk) may be doubling every 22 years, but its high-school graduate population has been doubling every four." By the mid-1970s, over 90 percent of the total school age population went to school, which was at that time one of the highest rates in the world for a developing area (Ballendorf 1977). These participation rates seemed to indicate that high school graduation rates would continue to increase in the near future.

The expansion of secondary school education lead to a massive surge into college that began in the 1970s. As the number of high school graduates in the TTPI increased, there was a growing interest in continuing studies in overseas universities, especially in the United States. However, government scholarship and college loan funds for tertiary education abroad were limited and, combined with the rapid increase of high school graduates, nearly exhausted by the early 1970s (Hezel and Levin 1990). In the late 1960s and early 1970s, only about 300 to 400 Micronesians were studying at universities outside of Micronesia, usually in Palau or Guam (Barringer, Gardner, and Levin 1993; Hezel and Levin 1990). However, in 1972, Micronesians were formally declared eligible for US federal education grants (Pell Grants) aimed at enabling the economically and socially disadvantaged to attend college. The number of Micronesians going to college overseas increased, with their primary destination shifting from Palau and Guam to the United States (Hezel and Levin 1990). The dramatic increase in emigration for university education has been best documented for Chuuk: about 900 Chuukese studied outside in 1973, 2,200 in 1975, and 3,000 in 1977 (Barringer, Gardner, and Levin 1993). The increase experienced in the remaining three states was probably equally as dramatic. By 1978, about 50 percent of all high school graduates from the FSM were attending college (Hezel and Levin 1990).

After the "Boom" Years

Given the limited economic opportunities in the villages, many of the college graduates who returned to the FSM in the 1970s migrated to the growing urban centers in search of employment. Even though the regular US subsidy peaked in the 1970s, other sources of US funding such as capital improvement grants were bringing in millions of dollars and hundreds of new jobs to Micronesia. The economy of the Trust Territory continued to grow through the 1970s, mostly through the expansion of the public sector. This infusion of additional funds into the public sector also induced a rise of employment in the private sector. The total number of jobs in the FSM more than doubled between 1970 and 1979 and, in general, returning college graduates could find jobs. However, following the declaration of self-government in 1979, strict budget ceilings were imposed on annual US grants and several Federal Programs that had employed hundreds of Micronesians were terminated. The employment figures of 1982 reflect the cutbacks in US funding. Overall, the FSM lost more than 1,700 jobs between

1979 and 1982, while about 1,800 graduates, half of them with some college education, entered the labor force. Chuuk and Yap suffered the most severe losses, losing 32 percent and 27 percent respectively of their 1979 job levels (Hezel and Levin 1990; Hezel and McGrath 1989).

There appears to have been two immediate responses to the shrinking economy of the early 1980s. First, there was a general reversal of the rural to urban migration experienced in the 1970s. This includes a reduction in the number of migrants moving from the outer islands to the main islands as well as an increase in the movement to outlying areas. This change was probably the result of outer islanders returning home to their villages rather than facing the increasing unemployment on the main islands (Gorenflo and Levin 1995; Hezel and Levin 1990). Second, there was a decline in school enrollments, in the number of high school graduates, and in the number high school graduates going on to college. Hezel and Levin (1990:54-56) discuss two reasons for this decline. For most Micronesian parents, schooling had represented an investment that would pay dividends when their children would qualify for salaried jobs and provide them financial security. As parents and students came to realize that employment was no longer the sure reward of twelve or more years of schooling, both the number of high school enrollments and graduates declined. Also, the rising cost of air travel and tuition put college beyond the means of many Micronesian families, even with federal assistance. Combined with the low probability of employment in the FSM after graduation, college became an increasingly risky investment. As a result, the primary destination of those who did pursue tertiary education shifted in the 1980s to locations closer to home, such as Guam or Hawaii, and the number of college-bound students declined. Many of those students who decided not to pursue additional formal education returned to their villages, which also helps explain the urban to rural migration that occurred in the 1980s (Gorenflo and Levin 1995).

The Compact of Free Association and Migration Beyond the FSM

The post-1945 social, political, and economic policies of the United States in the Pacific Trust Territories indirectly caused an increase in internal migration in the FSM. Three policies were especially important in creating this mobility. First, the infusion of funds by the United States and the development of a wage economy undermined the subsistence economy that predominated until the 1960s. This increased the importance of money, and by the 1970s, fewer and fewer households produced their own food, which increased the need for wage employment to obtain basic subsistence needs. Household members migrated to those growing urban centers where jobs were available. Second, the policy of universal education and the development of the education infrastructure lead to an education explosion in the 1970s, resulting in a dramatic increase in the number of high school and college graduates. Many Micronesians saw education as an investment that would lead to wage employment in the growing economy. Internal migration increased as students moved to education centers and as high school graduates and returning college graduates moved to find jobs. Finally, after the four states of the FSM declared independence, the US administration dramatically reduced the level of funds it channeled into the FSM economy. This caused the FSM economy to quickly shrink and resulted in both the loss of jobs as well as a decline in the number of jobs available. Rather than face the poor job prospects in urban centers, many former migrants returned to their home islands. This reversed the migration trends of the 1960s and 1970s and increased the level of urban-to-rural migration in the 1980s. Thus, these three policies of the United States government, although well-intentioned, helped create a population in the FSM that was increasingly wage-dependent, increasingly educated, increasingly unemployed or underemployed, and increasingly mobile. These trends created a population ripe for international migration.

Before independence and the signing of the Compact of Free Association, migration out of the FSM was generally limited to the other island countries of the TTPI. This changed when the Compact between the US and the FSM was implemented in 1986 and Micronesians for the first time were allowed free entry into the US and its territories. Also under the Compact, the United States agreed to provide annual subsidies, grant funds, and program assistance for fifteen years until 2001, while the FSM worked towards political development and economic independence. In exchange, the FSM guaranteed the United States exclusive use of its land for military purposes. However, the Micronesian negotiators of the Compact recognized that, even with this aid, it was unlikely the FSM would be able to generate the level of economic growth necessary to provide enough employment for its increasing population. It was for this reason that the negotiators insisted on a provision that would allow Micronesians to migrate freely to the United States and its territories and to live and work there indefinitely. Emigration to the United States was seen as a way to lessen the impact of rapid population growth as well as a safety valve if the plans to develop the islands economically failed (Hezel and McGrath 1989; Hezel and Levin 1990).

Within weeks after the signing of the Compact, whole families of Micronesians and especially young, single men began leaving the FSM for destinations overseas, mostly Guam and the CNMI (Rubinstein and Levin 1992). A number of leaders in both the FSM and Guam were shocked by how quickly so many people took advantage of the migration provision (Rubinstein and Levin 1992:150). However, perhaps this was not too surprising, given that the economic, education, and migration trends of the FSM since the 1960s, many indirectly generated by US policies, created a "surplus" population of increasingly educated, under-employed, and mobile individuals. Those who left immediately after the signing of the Compact may have already been planning and preparing to emigrate.

Micronesian Populations Overseas

Since early in the post-Compact period, the main destinations for FSM migrants have been to the CNMI and Guam. There were two reasons for this preference. First, during the late 1980s and through the 1990s, the economies of both Guam and the CNMI were expanding, mostly through the growth of tourism and other labor-intensive industries, while the economy of the FSM was contracting. Thus, one of the main reasons for migration from the FSM to these areas was employment. Initially, the migration stream was directed to the CNMI. Before the signing of the Compact, the CNMI was part of the TTPI and was a favorite destination for Micronesians seeking employment. After Compact implementation, Micronesians continued to migrate to the CNMI to reunite with family members and to find employment in the growing tourist and garment factory industries. However, these industries became increasingly dominated by foreign labor, most from Asia. As the competition for jobs increased and as wages relative to those available on Guam declined, Guam emerged as the primary destination for FSM migrants (Gorenflo and Levin 1995).[xii] Also, unlike the CNMI, Guam has severe restrictions on the importation of alien labor, so the FSM was seen by Guam businesses as the most likely source of labor for the growing tourist industry (Hezel and McGrath 1989). Rubinstein and Levin (1992:374-75) report that, in the early 1990s, several large hotels even recruited Micronesian workers in the FSM to fill the growing number of low-skill, entry-level positions available.

Second, both Guam and the CNMI are preferred destinations because of their close proximity to the FSM, especially relative to Hawaii and the US Mainland.[xii] Transportation between the FSM and Guam and the CNMI is relatively cheap and easy. This proximity enables many Micronesian migrants to return to the FSM for visits several times a year, thus maintaining strong social ties with their families and a strong cultural orientation (Hezel and McGrath 1989; Rubinstein and Levin 1992). This pattern of circular migration became so common that the migrants were seen as "virtually commuters" (FSM National Census Office 1996:153). Micronesians living in Hawaii and on the US Mainland have a more difficult time practicing circular migration because of the distances and costs involved (Barringer, Gardner, and Levin 1993).

Since Compact implementation, the population of the FSM migrants on Guam has steadily increased from 1,700 in 1988 (Hezel and Levin 1996) to 5,489 in 1997 (US Department of the Interior 1997). According to the US Census Bureau, there were 6,983 migrants born in the FSM residing in Guam in 2000 (US Census Bureau, Census 2000, Guam Summary File). The CNMI data is less certain, but it appears that the Micronesian migrant population initially increased and then began to decline in the early 1990s. In 1990, the migrant population in the CNMI was 1,754 and by 1993 the population increased to 2,261. By 1995, however, the population declined to 2,111 (Hezel and Levin 1996). Unfortunately, comparable national figures for the CNMI are not available for 1998. In 1998 there were 1,684 migrants from the FSM living on Saipan, the main island in the Northern Marianas group (US Department of the Interior 1998). Although not definitive, this may indicate a continuing decline in the total number of FSM migrants in CNMI. For Hawaii, only one estimate exists. In 1997, there were 2,338[xiv] migrants from the FSM living in Hawaii (US Department of the Interior 1997).[xv] According to 1990 US census data, there were 2,949 "other" Micronesians living on the US mainland, which would include those migrants from the FSM (Barringer, Gardner, and Levin 1993). Census 2000 reported that there were approximately 2,000 people who reported Chuukese, Kosraean, Pohnpeian, or Yapese as their race, but this number includes both migrants and native born (Grieco 2001).[xvi] The number of Micronesians in Hawaii and on the US mainland attest to the fact that most emigration from the FSM is to destinations closer to home.

In the immediate post-Compact period, the initial wave of Micronesian migrants to Guam consisted mostly of young, working-age males, a characteristic typical of labor migration flows. In 1989, a survey of the Micronesians on Guam showed that adult men outnumbered adult women nearly two-to-one (Rubinstein and Levin 1992). Many of the original households were inherently unstable, composed of several young men working at low-wage jobs and pooling income to cover rent and other expenses (Hezel and McGrath 1989:58-60). By the early 1990s, the age-sex structure of the migrant population on Guam was normalizing and beginning to resemble the age-sex structure of the home population (Rubinstein and Levin 1992). There is also evidence to suggest that, by 1994, households were incorporating members according to kinship principles, with grandparents and other older people being added, giving the households important generational depth (FSM National Census Office 1996:154).

By the mid-1990s, the FSM migrant households in the CNMI were rapidly filling out with dependents – women, children, and the elderly – and were rapidly moving towards the reconstitution of normal Micronesian households overseas. According to Hezel and Levin (1996:101), the CNMI migrant households were "farther along the road to normalization and stabilization" than the Guam households were by this time. This may be the result of the earlier pre-Compact movement of migrants to the CNMI and the later shift to Guam as the primary destination for the FSM migrants. This would mean that, by the early-to-mid 1990s, the households on the CNMI would have had on average longer settlement periods than the households on Guam, giving them more time to reconstitute overseas.

Unfortunately, little research has focused on the Micronesian migrant community in Hawaii. Anecdotal evidence suggests, however, that the migration flow to Hawaii is qualitatively different from the flow going to either Guam or the CNMI. It is generally believed that migration from the FSM to Hawaii began later than the migration to either Guam or the CNMI and that the primary motive is capital accumulation, either through immediate employment or employment after education, and not household reunification. If this is true then the migrant population of Hawaii may exhibit many of the characteristics of early labor flows, such as a high proportion of single, predominantly male individuals, few dependents per household (e.g., spouse, children, elderly), and a high proportion of non-family households. Given the distance between the FSM and Hawaii and the cost of transportation, whether or not the migrants proceed with household reconstitution in Hawaii will probably depend on their ability to balance the cost of living with the expense of supporting dependent relatives.

THE NATURE OF THE MIGRATION FLOWS FROM THE FSM
TO GUAM AND HAWAII

According to the migration history literature, the first significant emigration from the FSM began in the years following the implementation of the Compact of Free Association in 1986. Although the CNMI was the initial primary destination for FSM migrants, Guam quickly became the destination of choice because of superior employment opportunities. Although initially a labor migration flow, by the mid-1990s the FSM households on Guam were beginning to incorporate additional members based on Micronesian kinship principles. This appears to have signaled the beginning of a transition from a labor migration to a family-reunification flow. Although there is little research on the FSM migrant community in Hawaii, anecdotal evidence suggests that the migration flow is younger than the flow to Guam and is qualitatively different. The main goal of migrants to Hawaii is capital accumulation, either through immediate employment or employment after education, and the flow is dominated by young males with few dependents. These characteristics – the emphasis on employment, job skills, and capital accumulation and the dominance of male migrants – are attributes typically associated with labor flows in the early stage of movement. It may be that the migration flow to Hawaii is a labor flow that is simply too new to show signs of family reunification settlement.

The previous section described how the post-war policies of the United States government in the Pacific helped create the migration flows out of the FSM that established the Micronesian migrant communities in both Guam and Hawaii. This section describes some of the social, economic, and migration characteristics of the Micronesian communities in both Guam and Hawaii. This description has three objectives. First, as suggested by the migration history literature, it shows that the migration flow to Guam is older than the flow to Hawaii. Second, as also suggested by the migration history literature, it shows that the older migration flow to Guam is dominated by family reunification migration, while the younger flow to Hawaii exhibits characteristics of an early labor migration flow. Finally, it demonstrates that the households in Guam are larger and more established, financially and socially, than the households in Hawaii. The differences detailed in this section are important for this research because of the implications they have for household remittance behavior. Older, more financially stable migrant households in the middle-to-late stages of family reunification may be better able and more likely to remit than younger, financially unstable households at the beginning of the family reunification process. The analytical implications of these differences on household remittance behavior are further discussed at the end of this chapter.

The Age of the Migration Flows

There are a number of characteristics that suggest the migration flow to Guam is older than the flow to Hawaii. The clearest indication of this difference in age can be seen when the years the migrant households have been established overseas are compared. Table 4-1 shows the years overseas of the earliest migrant in the household, by average and five-year age group, for Guam and Hawaii. The years overseas of the earliest migrant is a proxy for household age, because it measures the maximum length of time the earliest migrant's household has been established overseas. As can be seen, households in Guam have been established overseas an average of about eight years, which is approximately a year and a half longer than the households in Hawaii. The overwhelming majority of the Guam households (approximately 80 percent) have been overseas five or more years, while almost half of the Hawaii households (45 percent) have been overseas less than five years. Only 8 percent of all households in Guam have been established less than two years, while over one-fourth of all Hawaii migrant households have been established overseas for the same length of time.

The difference in the age of the migration flows is also reflected in the years the individual migrants have spent overseas. Table 4-1 also shows the years overseas of all migrants, by average and five-year groups, for Guam and Hawaii. Migrants in Guam have been overseas

**Table 4-1:   Years Overseas of All Migrants and Earliest Migrants by
Average and Five-Year Groups, Guam and Hawaii, 1997**

Characteristic	Years	Percent or Mean	
		Guam	**Hawaii**
Average Years Overseas, Earliest Migrants		7.67	6.24
Years Overseas, Earliest Migrants, by Age	0 to 4	19.02	45.43
of Earliest Migrant (Five Year Groups)	5 to 9	57.33	36.68
	10 to 14	18.27	10.91
	15 and over	5.38	6.98
Average Years Overseas, All Migrants		4.84	4.22
Years Overseas, All Migrants, by Age of	0 to 4	49.39	65.13
Migrant (Five-Year Groups)	5 to 9	43.08	26.32
	10 to 14	6.23	5.35
	15 and over	1.30	3.21

longer than migrants in Hawaii, but the difference is minimal and not
statistically significant. However, a much larger proportion of migrants
arrived in Hawaii within the five years prior to the Micronesian Census,
again indicating an older flow to Guam. Approximately 65 percent of
all migrants to Hawaii arrived less than five years earlier, compared to
49 percent of all migrants to Guam. About 44 percent of the Hawaii
migrants arrived within just two years prior to the survey compared to
30 percent of the Guam migrants.

The differences in the age of the migration flows are best seen
graphically. Figure 4-1 shows the proportion of migrant households by
their years overseas for both Guam and Hawaii. The highest proportion
of migrant households established in Guam occurred in 1990, while the
highest proportion for Hawaii occurred seven years later in 1997. For
Guam, the proportion of migrant households established began to
increase a few years before Compact implementation in 1986, peaking
in 1990, when it began to decline continuously, again reaching pre-
Compact proportion levels in 1997. In Hawaii, the proportion of
migrant households established increased between 1987 and 1990, and

like Guam, peaked and began to decline. Unlike Guam, however, the graph shows evidence of a second surge of household establishment beginning in Hawaii in about 1992 and continuing until 1997. This second surge helps explain the much higher proportion of households established in Hawaii than Guam in the five years prior to the survey. A large percentage of the households in Hawaii were established after the peak years of household establishment in Guam, suggesting Hawaii is a younger migration flow.

Figure 4-2 shows the proportion of migrants by their years overseas for both Guam and Hawaii. As with the proportion of established households, the proportion of migrants arriving in both Guam and Hawaii increases after Compact implementation in 1986, peaks in 1990, and begins to decline. Unlike the proportion of established households, where only Hawaii experienced a second surge of household establishment, the graph shows that both Guam and Hawaii experienced a second, post-1990 surge of in-migration. This is especially evident in Hawaii. Clearly, while a high proportion of

Figure 4-1:   Proportion of FSM Migrant Households by Years Overseas, Guam and Hawaii, 1997

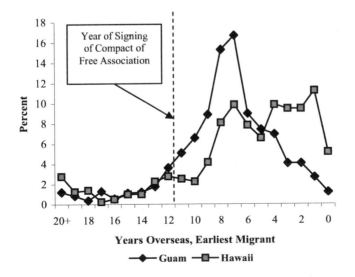

**Figure 4-2:   Proportion of FSM Migrants by Years Overseas,
                 Guam and Hawaii, 1997**

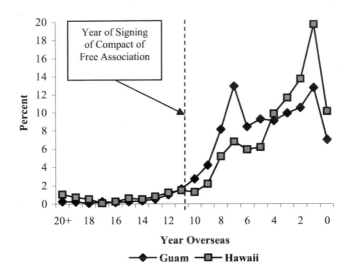

migrants in both communities arrived within the five years prior to the
survey, a much higher proportion of Hawaii than Guam migrants are
new arrivals. This again supports the view that the flow to Hawaii is a
younger migration flow.

Significance of the Age of the Migration Flows for Remittance Behavior

The changes in both the proportions of migrant households and in-
migrants through time indicate that the migration flow to Hawaii is
younger than the flow to Guam and consists of a higher proportion of
both newly established households and newly arrived migrants. The
difference in the age of the migration flows is significant because
Guam, as an older migrant community, exhibits certain characteristics
that could positively influence its aggregate remittance behavior,
making the probability of remitting higher than in Hawaii. These

include 1) higher levels of continued in-migration and family reunification and 2) larger, more socially and financially established households.

Evidence of continued migration and family reunification

Anecdotal evidence suggests that the migration flow to Hawaii is a labor migration flow in the early stages of movement. The Hawaii migrant community does show a number of characteristics that are indicative of a labor migration flow, including a high proportion of young, unmarried male migrants living with few dependents. Table 4-2 describes the age, sex, and marital characteristics of the migrants. In general, table 4-2 indicates few differences between the Guam and Hawaii migrant communities. On average, both communities are young, in their mid-20s, concentrated in the economically active age groups, and mostly unmarried. However, compared to Guam, the migrants in Hawaii are more likely to be older, male, single, and in the 15 to 29 age category. Also, migrants in Hawaii are less likely to live in households with dependents. A much lower proportion of the migrants in Hawaii is less than age 15, indicating fewer migrant children. Although both communities exhibit characteristics of a migration flow, the characteristics demonstrated by the migrants to Hawaii are more extreme. When combined with the lower level of dependents in the household – and the younger age of the migration stream, as discussed in the previous section – this provides initial evidence that the flow to Hawaii is an early-stage labor migration flow with little family reunification.

Although the age, sex, and marital characteristics of the Guam and Hawaii migrant communities are generally comparable, their household characteristics are quite different. These differences suggest the flow to Guam has been dominated by family reunification migration that, through the years, has produced a high proportion of family households with great kinship depth. Tables 4-3 through 4-5 provide descriptive statistics on various demographic, structural, and social characteristics of the FSM migrant households in both Guam and Hawaii. Generally

Table 4-2:   Age, Sex, and Marital Status Characteristics of the FSM Migrants, Guam and Hawaii, 1997

Characteristic		Percent, Ratio, or Mean	
		Guam	Hawaii
Sex Ratio		105.05	124.59
Mean Age		25.53	26.34
Age	Under 15 Years	21.50	15.61
	15 to 29 Years	44.88	52.61
	30 to 44 Years	25.08	22.67
	45 to 59 Years	6.73	6.12
	60 Years and Over	1.81	2.99
Marital Status of Persons	Never Married	57.60	59.79
Age 15 and Over	Married	26.27	28.53
	Consensually Married	12.62	7.10
	Widowed, Separated, or Divorced	3.51	4.58

Table 4-3:   Demographic and Structural Characteristics of FSM Migrant Households, Guam and Hawaii, 1997

Household Characteristic		Percent or Mean	
		Guam	Hawaii
Household Size		6.43	3.44
Dependency Ratio		59.42	41.06
Family Type	Family Household	96.67	65.22
	Married Couple	69.84	35.42
	Male Householder, No Wife	9.71	17.87
	Female Householder, No Husband	17.11	12.92
	Non-Family Households	3.33	34.78
Presence of Sub-Families	No Sub-Families	76.69	90.46
	One or More Sub-Families	23.31	9.54
Relation of Sub-Family	Child/Stepchild/Grandchild	19.48	8.10
Members to Household	Sibling or Parents	13.24	25.71
Head	Other Relative	67.28	66.19

Table 4-4:   Presence of Various Relatives of Earliest Migrant in FSM Migrant Households, Guam and Hawaii, 1997

Household Characteristic		Percent	
		Guam	Hawaii
Spouse		60.09	30.08
Parents	None	92.84	96.03
	One or Both	7.16	3.97
Children	None	34.50	66.06
	One or More	65.50	33.94
Grandchildren	None	95.60	97.95
	One or More	4.40	2.05
Siblings	None	78.99	89.41
	One or More	21.01	10.59
Other Relatives	None	45.23	65.58
	One or More	54.77	34.42

Table 4-5:   Kinship Depth of FSM Migrant Households, Guam and Hawaii, 1997

Household Characteristic	Percent	
	Guam	Hawaii
Migrant Living Alone or with Non-Relatives	4.36	38.05
Migrant Living with Spouse, Child(ren), or Spouse and Child(ren)	56.22	44.12
Migrant Living with Spouse, Child(ren) or Spouse and Child(ren), and Other Relatives	39.42	17.82

speaking, Guam households are larger, have more dependents, are much more likely to be family households, especially married-couple households, and are more likely to include one or more sub-families. Consequently, migrants in Guam are more much more likely to live with close relatives than are migrants in Hawaii. This includes immediate family members as well as more lateral kin. A higher percentage of Guam households include the spouse, children, grandchildren, parents, siblings, and other more distant relatives of the earliest migrant. Guam households are also more likely to have greater kinship depth. Almost 40 percent of all households on Guam include members of both the earliest migrants' nuclear family as well as members of his/her more extended family. Only 18 percent of the Hawaii households include both nuclear and extended family members. Less than 5 percent of the households on Guam consist of the migrant alone or with non-relatives, compared to 38 percent of the households in Hawaii.

The higher proportion of related individuals in the Guam migrant households is partially the result of a higher level of continued in-migration of new household members. Table 4-6 shows the migration characteristics of the FSM migrant households in Guam and Hawaii. When compared to Hawaii, Guam has a higher proportion of households with a latest arriving migrant. It also has a higher proportion of households that received additional migrants between the arrival times of the earliest and latest migrants. Over 51 percent of Guam households have received additional migrants, compared to only 32 percent of the Hawaii households. Guam households are not only more likely to receive additional migrants, but are more likely to receive more of them. On average, Guam households have received two additional members compared to the one additional member received by Hawaii households. These statistics suggest that the FSM migrant households on Guam have experienced a higher level of continued in-migration than Hawaii households. There is evidence to suggest that the majority of this continued migration to Guam is family reunification migration. Approximately 80 percent of all Guam migrant households have family members who migrated in different years, compared to only 48 percent of the migrant households in Hawaii. A large percentage of the Hawaii migrant households (43 percent) are single migrant households, indicating a comparatively low level of family reunification.

Table 4-6:   Migration Characteristics of FSM Migrant Households, Guam and Hawaii, 1997

Characteristic		Percent or Mean	
		Guam	Hawaii
Number of Years between Time of Arrival of Earliest and Latest Migrants		4.73	3.48
Number of Additional Migrants Arriving between Arrival Time of Earliest and Latest Migrants		1.73	0.76
Proportion of All Households with:	Latest Migrant	80.71	54.24
	Migrants Arriving between Arrival Time of Earliest and Latest Migrants	51.21	32.49
Proportion of All Households with:	No Additional In-Migrations	17.35	43.49
	One Additional In-Migration	31.45	24.02
	Two or More Additional In-Migrations	51.20	32.49
Family Reunification	Earliest Migrant and All Relatives in Household Migrated in Same Year	0.14	0.09
	Earliest Migrant and at Least One Relative in Household Migrated in Different Years	0.80	0.48
	Single Migrant in Household, Alone or with Non-Relative	0.06	0.43

The social and financial stability of Guam households

The characteristics of the Guam and Hawaii households indicate that the processes of continued and family reunification migration are less clear in the Hawaii migrant community. There are three reasons why this is so. First, the migration flow to Hawaii is younger than the flow to Guam, and the average age of the Guam migrant households is higher. As a result, the households in Hawaii have been established overseas for a shorter period of time. This decreases the time between the arrival of the earliest and latest migrants and thus decreases the relative likelihood that a new migrant member would have been incorporated into the household.

Second, the process of family reunification may be more evident in Guam because the migration flow is more "mature." The movement to Guam appears to have passed through the initial labor migration stage, which is typically dominated by young, male, single migrants, and into the family reunification stage, which has a higher proportion of female and dependent children migrants. Hawaii still shows many of the characteristics associated with a labor migration flow, especially the dominance of male migrants. This can be clearly seen in table 4-7, which shows the sex ratios by year of arrival. For Guam, males clearly dominated the pre-Compact migration flow as well as the first five years after Compact implementation, the time of the initial surge of FSM migration into Guam. After 1992 and until the year of the survey, female migrants dominate or equal males in the migration flow. This may indicate that the initial labor migration flow, which was dominated by males, has shifted to a family reunification flow, in which women and children typically predominate. The sex ratios by year of arrival for Hawaii show that males have dominated both the pre-Compact and post-Compact flows. This includes the five years before the survey, the time period in which approximately 65 percent of all FSM migrants to Hawaii arrived. This supports the view that the flow to Hawaii is a male-dominated labor flow that has not yet made the transition to family reunification migration.

Finally, the process of chain migration and family reunification may also be more evident in Guam because the households are simply more financially established and can afford to sponsor the migration of relatives. The majority of the migrants in Hawaii are new arrivals, arriving overseas less than five years before the survey, whereas a large proportion of the Guam migrants arrived between five and ten years earlier. This lower average number of years overseas would mean the

Table 4-7:   Sex Ratios by Year of Arrival, FSM Migrants, Guam and
              Hawaii, 1997

Year of Arrival	Sex Ratio	
	Guam	Hawaii
1997	91.13	125.71
1996	100.28	121.63
1995	100.00	137.78
1994	87.71	121.14
1993	98.03	111.93
1992	99.61	145.76
1991	102.16	104.41
1990	111.54	87.06
1989	146.45	124.07
1988	108.93	121.74
1987	118.84	100.00
Before 1986	138.74	170.15
All Migrants	105.05	123.41

migrants to Hawaii would have had less time to establish the base
households necessary to start the processes of chain migration and
family reunification. Also, a large percentage of the new arrivals in
Hawaii are establishing their own households, while the new arrivals to
Guam are joining the households already established by their families.
Newer households are more likely to be working to achieve financial
stability and may be less likely to have the resources available to
commit to family reunification. This may help explain the high
proportion of non-family households in Hawaii. Over one-third of all
migrant households in Hawaii consist of a migrant living alone or with
non-relatives (see table 4-5). The position of the migrants in the wider
Hawaii economy has probably also delayed the beginning of the family
reunification process. Table 4-8 shows the income, expenditure, and
labor force characteristics of FSM migrant households in Guam and
Hawaii. Compared to the Hawaii migrant households, Guam
households make less income and have fewer members in the labor
force but have more available resources. This apparently reflects the
higher cost of living in Hawaii. On a per capita basis, the migrants in

Table 4-8:   Income, Expenditure, and Labor Force Characteristics of FSM Migrant Households, Guam and Hawaii, 1997

Household Characteristic	Mean	
	Guam	Hawaii
Household Income	18,334.08	17,563.56
Per Capita	2,851.33	5,105.69
Household Members Age 16 to 64:		
In Labor Force	2.35	1.34
Worked for Pay in 1996	1.81	1.19
Percent of Household Members:		
In Labor Force	39.14	44.05
Worked for Pay in 1996	31.18	40.69
Family Poverty Status(a)	82.22	75.16
Household Monthly Maintenance Expenditure	702.32	792.48
Per Capita	109.23	230.37
Household Maintenance as Percent of Household Income	11.03	18.75

(a) A value of 100 on the family poverty status would mean the family is living just above the poverty level (or "threshold"). This means that, on average, Micronesian migrant families in both Guam and Hawaii are living below the poverty threshold. However, Hawaii migrant households have a lower family poverty status than do Guam migrant households. This means the Hawaii migrants are, on average, living in more severe poverty.

Hawaii spend more to maintain their households than Guam migrants do. Hawaii households also have a higher percentage of adult migrant members in the labor force and a lower family poverty status. The higher cost of living may partially explain the higher proportion of non-family households and the higher likelihood that the earliest migrant will live with either a more distant relative or a non-relative in Hawaii. Newly arrived migrants may be forming households with friends and distant relatives in an effort to cut costs.

There is additional evidence that shows the Hawaii migrants are forming households with more distant kin before immediate kin. Table

4-9 shows the mean years overseas of migrant household members as they are related to the earliest migrant. It also shows the results of the difference of means t-tests comparing the mean years overseas of the earliest migrant with other household members. On Guam, the mean years overseas are clearly "stacked," with the earliest migrant arriving overseas before all other members of the household, followed sequentially by his/her spouse, children, sibling, and parents and other relatives and non-relatives. This "stacked" pattern is supported by the results of the t-tests. While not definitive, this pattern in the data does suggest that a process of chain migration, where a migrant is joined first by immediate relatives and later by more distant relatives, is occurring in the migrant households on Guam.

However, a "stacked" pattern is less clear in the Hawaii data. In the Hawaii migrant households, the earliest migrant arrives first, followed by his/her spouse and then children. Unlike Guam households, in the Hawaii households other relatives and non-relatives arrive on average before the earliest migrants' parents and siblings.[xvii] This may also be because of the higher cost of living in Hawaii. Micronesian households in Hawaii may need a larger "critical mass" of workers – not dependents – for household survival. When compared to Guam households, the Hawaii households do have a higher proportion of their adult migrant members in the labor force, with personal income, and who worked for pay in the previous year (see table 4-8). Hawaii households may be incorporating more distant relatives and non-relatives rather than siblings and parents because they are less likely to be dependents and may be more likely to contribute to the economy of the household. This supports the view that the Hawaii migration flow is a labor flow still in the early stages of movement. The evidence for chain and family reunification migration is low because the migrants are just beginning the process of household reconstitution by incorporating more distant relatives into their newly established households.

Table 4-9: Difference of Means T-Tests Comparing the Mean Years Overseas of the Earliest Migrant and Related Household Members, Guam and Hawaii, 1997

Relationship to Earliest Migrant	Mean Years Overseas	T-Value and Significance Level					
		Earliest Migrant	Spouse	Child/Stepchild	Sibling	Parent	Other Relative
Guam							
1. Earliest Migrant	7.63	--	--	--	--	--	--
2. Spouse	6.00	8.73 ***	--	--	--	--	--
3. Child/Stepchild	4.89	18.96 ***	7.60 ***	--	--	--	--
4. Sibling	3.78	18.02 ***	11.58 ***	6.94 ***	--	--	--
5. Parent	3.81	9.68 ***	6.69 ***	3.82 ***	-0.09 ns	--	--
6. Other Relative	3.31	34.86 ***	20.67 ***	15.57 ***	3.21 ***	1.86 *	--
7. Non-Relative	3.12	14.98 ***	11.42 ***	8.12 ***	2.82 **	2.24 *	0.91 ns
Hawaii							
1. Earliest Migrant	6.22	--	--	--	--	--	--
2. Spouse	4.92	3.32 ***	--	--	--	--	--
3. Child/Stepchild	3.85	7.04 ***	3.34 ***	--	--	--	--
4. Sibling	2.06	8.30 ***	8.05 ***	4.99 ***	--	--	--
5. Parent	1.64	5.65 ***	6.26 ***	4.03 ***	1.12 ns	--	--
6. Other Relative	2.77	14.92 ***	8.76 ***	4.89 ***	-2.45 **	-2.50 **	--
7. Non-Relative	3.14	7.54 ***	5.69 ***	2.32 *	-3.59 ***	-3.65 ***	-1.51 ns

Note: * p<.05; ** p<.01; *** p<.001

Implications for Household Remittance Behavior

The descriptive data presented in this chapter suggests that, when compared to Hawaii, the migration flow to Guam is older and dominated by family reunification migration to older, more established households. Hawaii has a higher proportion of single-migrant households, newly arrived migrants, and newly established households that indicate the flow to Hawaii is younger than that to Guam. What are the implications of these differences for household remittance behavior? For Guam, there are two possibilities. First, if the households in Guam that exhibit the characteristics associated with continued migration are currently in the family reunification process, they may still have dependent members overseas and a high probability of remitting. However, if the majority of households have already completed the family reunification process and all of the dependent family members from overseas have already been brought to Guam, there will be no one left to remit to in the FSM and remittances levels will be low or non-existent. Given the characteristics of the migration flow to Guam, it is most likely that Guam migrant households are in the middle of the family reunification process and are actively remitting.

Second, the relatively low cost of living in Guam coupled with the higher number of workers per household could mean that Guam households generate enough discretionary income to be able to remit, possibly at high levels. For Hawaii, the majority of the migrants are young, single, and newly arrived, either living in non-family households or households that lack kinship depth. Combined with the effects of the higher cost of living in Hawaii, these households may not generate enough discretionary income or be in the economic position to remit. However, because the migration flow to Hawaii is relatively "young," it is more likely that households in Hawaii than in Guam still have dependent members in the FSM. In this sense, even though the Hawaii migrants may still be in the early stages of household establishment and may be less able economically to remit, they may be more motivated to do so. This may mean that the probability of remitting will be higher in Hawaii than in Guam. It may also mean that the relationship between household income and the amount remitted, rather than being linear and positive, becomes obscured. This is because at the early stage of household reunification and reformation overseas, it is not the total household income that determines the amount remitted, but the proportion of immediate kin in the country of origin and the subsequent motivation of the migrants within the household to remit.

This chapter presented a brief history of the Federates States of Micronesia and the establishment of the Micronesian migrant communities in Guam and Hawaii. This provided the contextual historic information necessary to fully understand the generation of the migration flows that established both communities. This chapter then described several characteristics of the migrant communities and their households, placing emphasis on three key comparative issues: the age of the migration flows, the amount of continued migration and family reunification, and the social and economic stability of the households. This demonstrated that, when compared to Hawaii, the migration flow to Guam is older and dominated by family reunification migration to older, well-established homes. Hawaii has a higher proportion of single-migrant households, newly arrived migrants, and newly established households that also indicate the flow to Hawaii is younger than that to Guam. As I will show in later chapters, these characteristics are significant because they help explain some of the differences found in the Guam and Hawaii statistical analyses in chapters five through seven. The next chapter details the development of a "baseline" model that analyzes the influence of time and resources on remittance behavior. By modeling remittance behavior at the household, rather than the individual, analytical level, the results of the "baseline" analysis show that both the likelihood (log odds) of remitting and the amount remitted exhibit evidence of remittance decay. This provides support for the remittance decay hypothesis.

CHAPTER 5

Time, Resources, and Remittance Behavior

Fundamental to the any study of remittance duration is, of course, a measure of time. Equally fundamental is a measure of the financial resources available for remitting, because it is the availability of these resources that ultimately determines whether or not remittances are sent overseas. The remittance literature includes quantitative studies focusing on a wide range of themes, such as the characteristics and determinants of remittance behavior (Banerjee 1984; Funkhouser 1995; Hoddinott 1992; Johnson and Whitelaw 1974; Knowles and Anker 1981; Lucas and Stark 1985; Menjivar et al. 1999; Stark and Lucas 1988), the influence of remittances on income distribution and development in the country of origin (Durand et al. 1996; Massey and Basem 1992; Rempel and Lobdell 1978), and analyses of a single issue, such as the influence of the passage of time (Brown 1997, 1998). Regardless of this diversity, almost all remittance studies, especially those focusing on the characteristics and determinants of remittance behavior, include measures of both time and resources. This pattern underscores the importance of these variables in remittance research.

Although most remittance research includes measures of both time and resources, these variables are often measured at different analytical levels than the dependent variable(s) used in the analyses. Because of restrictions presented by the various data sets used in remittance studies, researchers are often forced to use dependent and explanatory variables measured at different analytical levels, even when they would prefer not to (see Menjivar et al. 1998:123). For example, most data sets collect information about the amount of remittances sent by the household rather than the amount sent by individual household members. However, the goal of most remittance research is to explain individual, not household, remittance behavior. This is probably the main reason why remittance duration is universally measured as an individual-level variable. Yet, data restrictions may also play a role. In many of the data sets used in remittance studies, detailed individual-level information is collected on only a single household member. This effectively prevents the creation of a household-level time variable based on the migration information of all household members. The lack of detailed information on each migrant also appears to influence the analytical level of the income variable. While some studies are able to derive the time and income information from the same migrant household member, the majority of studies incorporate a combination of individual- and household-level income variables to explain individual remittance behavior.

As outlined in chapter three, the sociological approach to remittance behavior suggests that it is a household rather than an individual-level phenomenon. In this research, I avoid the analytical "schizophrenia" often found in other studies by modeling remittance behavior solely at the household level. That is, both my dependent and explanatory variables are modeled at the same analytical level. Fortunately, the Census of Micronesian Migrants does not have many of the same restrictions of other data sets used in remittance research. The Micronesian Census includes both household and individual-level data, including information on the demographic, income, and migration characteristics of all members of the FSM (Federated States of Micronesia) households. The individual-level migration data are especially important because they make possible innovative measures of both time and income not previously used in remittance research, measures that are consistent with a sociological approach to remittance behavior. Specifically, to measure remittance duration, the time overseas of the earliest migrant is used. As the first migrant in the household, the years overseas of the earliest migrant reflects the length of time since the migrant household was established. Also, an adult equivalent income is used to measure household financial resources. Unlike traditional income measures, the adult equivalent income accounts for both household resources as well as need by adjusting for household size, composition, and economies of scale.

Because of the importance of time and income in remittance research, this chapter focuses on developing a simple "baseline" model using these two basic determinants of remittance behavior. It begins by reviewing how time and income are traditionally measured in the remittance literature. It then describes the alternative measures of time and resources used in this research and explains why these alternative measures are better for analyzing remittance behavior than those traditionally used. The results of the baseline analyses are also presented. They show that when time is modeled at the household level, both the probability of remitting[xviii] and the amount remitted decline through time, lending support to the remittance decay hypothesis.

MEASURING REMITTANCE DURATION

In the remittance literature, time is always measured at the level of the individual, regardless of the analytical level of the dependent variable. Table 5-1 summarizes the measures of remittances and remittance duration used in several studies focusing on both internal (Banerjee 1984; Hoddinott 1982; Johnson and Whitelaw 1974; Knowles and Anker 1981) and international migrants (Brown 1997, 1998; Funkhouser 1995; Menjivar et al. 1998). Usually, remittance duration is measured as the time the migrant household head or a random individual within the household (e.g., main migrant respondent) has been living away from home, either overseas or in an urban area. Several of the earlier studies (Banerjee 1984; Johnson and Whitelaw 1974; Knowles and Anker 1981) even restricted their measures of time to male migrants only. Most of these studies also assume, or at least test for, a non-linear (quadratic) relationship between remittance

Table 5-1: Summary of Measures of Remittances and Remittance Duration Used in the Remittance Literature

Author(s)	Measures		Significance of Remittance Duration Variables
	Remittances (Dependent Variable(s))	Remittance Duration	
Banerjee (1984)	Whether or not the household has remitted; the amount of money remitted per month	Number of months of residence in urban area of male migrant household head plus quadratic term	Tobit: Time and time-squared not significant. Probit: Time (+) significant, time-squared not significant. OLS: Time (-) and time-squared (+) significant.
Brown (1997, 1998)	Dollar value of remittances (both cash and goods) sent by the household overseas in 12 months prior to survey	Number of months since the migrant head of household emigrated plus quadratic term	Tobit: Time and time-squared not significant.
Funkhouser (1995)	Whether or not the household has received remittances from the migrant; the amount received from migrant	Number of years since the emigration of the migrant household member plus quadratic term	*Salvadoran households:* Tobit: Time (-) significant, time-squared not significant. Probit: Time significant (-), time squared not significant. OLS: Time not significant, time-squared (+) significant. *Nicaraguan households:* Tobit: Time (-) and time-squared (+) significant. Probit: Time (-) and time-squared (+) significant. OLS: Time and time-squared not significant.

Table 5-1: Summary of Measures of Remittances and Remittance Duration Used in the Remittance Literature (Continued)

Author(s)	Measures		Significance of Remittance Duration Variables
	Remittances (Dependent Variable(s))	Remittance Duration	
Hoddinott (1982)	Whether or not migrant remitted in the 12 months prior to the survey; the amount remitted by migrant per month	Dummy variables: whether or not the migrant has been in the urban area for more than one year and for more than two years	Tobit: Time significant. Probit: Time significant when year>1 but not when year>2. OLS: Time not significant.
Johnson and Whitelaw (1974)	Proportion of monthly income remitted by migrant to rural area	Years of urban residence of male migrant respondent	OLS: Time (+) significant.
Knowles and Anker (1981)	Whether or not the household remitted; the amount of remittances sent by the household during preceding year	Years male migrant head of household has resided away from home; also tested quadratic term	Logistic: Time (-) significant, time-squared not significant. OLS: Time and time-squared not significant.
Menjivar et al. (1998)	Whether or not the household remitted; the amount of remittances sent by the household overseas during the year before the survey	Years overseas of the main migrant respondent; also tested quadratic term	Logistic: Time (-) significant, time-squared not significant. OLS: Time and time-squared not significant.

Note: Signs in parentheses in column 4 indicate sign of coefficient.

behavior and time, as suggested by Stark's remittance decay hypothesis (see chapter two, figure 2-1). The results of these studies provide, at best, limited support for either a quadratic or linear relationship between remittance behavior and time, as can be seen in table 5-1.

One reason why the remittance decay hypothesis has received so little support in the literature may be because of the analytical level (i.e., at the level of the individual) traditionally used to measure time. In this study, remittance duration is measured as the number of years the earliest migrant in the household has been overseas. While this is technically an individual-level variable, it is a better measure of remittance duration than the years overseas of the household head (or a random migrant respondent) for two reasons. First, the year of arrival by the earliest migrant marks the point in time when the earliest migrant's household was established overseas. This is important, because for those households that receive additional migrants through time, it marks the earliest point in time when the process of continued migration and family reunification began.

Second, the years overseas of the earliest migrant measures the maximum length of time that the migrant's household has been overseas. When remittance duration is measured using the time overseas of the household head (or a random individual within the household) it is not known whether that individual is the earliest migrant, the latest migrant, or somewhere in between. Using the years overseas of the household head, without knowing the relation of his or her migration history to the other members of the household, can minimize the effect of time on remittance behavior because it can cut short the period of time (see figure 5-1). This would be especially true if the household head, for some cultural or other reason, is normally not the earliest migrant in the household. For example, if wives normally migrate before husbands, but males are normatively defined as the head of the household, the time overseas of the household head would not accurately reflect the length of the *household* has been established overseas. It would instead reflect the length of time an *individual within*

Figure 5-1: Illustration of "Household Time," the Time Overseas of the Earliest Migrant, Compared to "Householder Time," the Time Overseas of the Householder

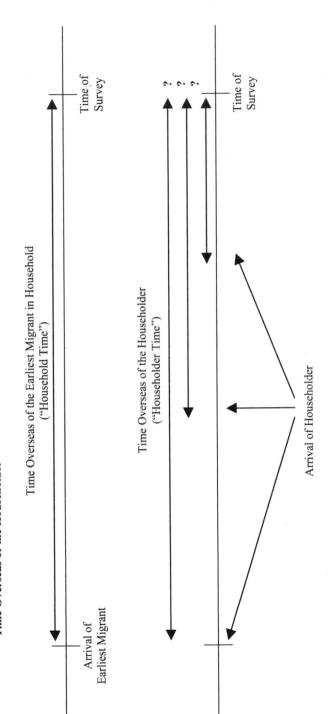

the household has been overseas. Because the years overseas of the earliest migrant measures the maximum number of years that a household has been established overseas, it is theoretically a better measure of household remittance duration, or "household time."

Householder Time vs. Household Time

Is household time a better measure of remittance duration than the individual level measures used by other researchers? Not only is the years overseas of the earliest migrant a better measure of remittance duration for theoretical reasons (see chapter 3), there is also evidence that, in some cases, it may be a more accurate measure of time. Table 5-2 shows the results of the logistic and OLS regression analyses using the time overseas of the householder[xix] and the time overseas of the earliest migrant. In the Guam logistic analyses, both remittance duration and its square are significant when the years overseas of the earliest migrant is used, but both are insignificant when the years overseas of the householder is used. In the Guam OLS analyses, only remittance duration is significant when household time is used, but neither remittance duration nor its square are significant when householder time is used. Unlike Guam, in the Hawaii logistic and OLS analyses, both measures of remittance duration perform equally as well.

The reason why household time is a better measure of remittance duration than householder time in Guam is probably due to the difference in the average years spent overseas by the earliest migrant and the migrant householder. On average, the migrant householder has been overseas about one year less than the earliest migrant.[xx] By cutting time short, householder time has the statistical effect of reducing the size of the regression coefficients, but not the standard errors. This results in less significant (or insignificant) duration variables.

The migrant householder in Hawaii has also been overseas about one year less than the earliest migrant, so this does not explain why the results of both remittance duration measurements are so consistent in

Table 5-2: Comparison of Duration Models Using Years Overseas of the Householder ("Householder Time") and Years Overseas of the Earliest Migrant ("Household Time"), Guam and Hawaii, 1997

Statistical Model	Guam		Hawaii	
	Time Overseas, Householder	Time Overseas, Earliest Migrant	Time Overseas, Householder	Time Overseas, Earliest Migrant
Likelihood of Remitting (logistic regression)	N=1,070	N=1,078	N=778	N=789
Intercept	-0.737***	-1.153***	-1.237***	-1.332***
Remittance Duration	0.057	0.130***	0.232***	0.235***
Remittance Duration, Squared	-0.002	-0.005**	-0.009***	-0.010***
Log Likelihood	1,415.5	1,416.2	998.2	1,013.1
Amount Remitted (OLS regression)	N=402	N=403	N=300	N=302
Intercept	5.443***	5.316***	5.996***	5.829***
Remittance Duration	0.045	0.069*	-0.041	0.010
Remittance Duration, Squared	-0.002	-0.003	0.002	0.000
R-squared	0.006	0.008	0.004	0.004

*Significant at p<.10. **Significant at p<.05. ***Significant at p<.01.

the Hawaii analyses. The consistency of the results is probably due to certain characteristics of the Hawaii FSM households and in the migration flow. Specifically, Hawaii households are smaller and have been established overseas for fewer years than the Guam households have, and the migration flow to Hawaii is a younger flow. These characteristics have the effect of reducing the differences between the householder and the earliest migrant. This occurs in three ways. First, because the households in Hawaii are younger households, there is less difference between the time of arrival of the earliest migrant and all other migrants in the household.[xxi] This means that, on average, there will be less difference in the time spent overseas by the earliest migrant and the migrant household member designated as the householder. Second, because the Hawaii households are smaller and have fewer migrants than the Guam households, there is a greater probability that the householder, or the migrant randomly chosen as the main respondent, is also the earliest migrant. There is some evidence in the Micronesian Census data that this has occurred. In Hawaii, 78 percent of the householders are also the earliest migrants, compared to 74 percent in Guam. Finally, the higher proportion of householders in Hawaii who are also the earliest migrants increases the overlap between the two samples and reduces the difference between the two measures of remittance duration. Combined, these characteristics reduce the differences between the earliest migrant and the householder and increase the similarities in the statistical analyses.

The results of the comparison of the duration models show that measuring time at the level of the household is not only preferable theoretically but empirically as well. While the Hawaii analyses indicate that there are circumstances where either duration measurement will provide the same results, the Guam analyses clearly demonstrate that this is not always the case. Householder time has the effect of reducing the influence of time on remittance behavior by reducing the average length of remittance duration, especially in older migration flows. Household time, because it is a more accurate measure of the number of years the migrant household has been established overseas, maximizes the period of remittance duration. This increases the likelihood that, if time does indeed influence remittance behavior, it will be statistically significant in the regression analyses. The results of the comparison between householder and household time may also help explain why few studies using an individual level measure of remittance duration have found that it significantly influences remittance behavior.

MEASURING FINANCIAL RESOURCES

Compared to the measures of time in the remittance literature, there is more variability in the way researchers measure the financial resources available for remitting. Almost all studies include a measure of income. Table 5-3 summarizes the measures of remittances and income used in several studies on both internal and international migration. Income is usually measured as either the monthly or annual income of the household (Banerjee 1984; Brown 1998; Knowles and Anker 1981; Menjivar et al. 1998), although a few individual-level studies use the migrant's monthly earnings (Hoddinott 1982; Johnson and Whitelaw 1974). Some studies include other household assets besides income that would increase the resources available for remitting, such as savings (Brown 1998), home ownership (Knowles and Anker 1981; Menjivar et al. 1998), and land ownership (Banerjee 1984; Hoddinott 1982; Johnson and Whitelaw 1974). A number of studies also include characteristics of the main migrant respondent that could increase household resources. The most common characteristic included is the years of education of the main migrant respondent (Banerjee 1984; Funkhouser 1995; Hoddinott 1982; Johnson and Whitelaw 1974; Knowles and Anker 1981), but labor force characteristics, such as employment status or hours worked per week, have also been included (Funkhouser 1995; Menjivar et al. 1998).

Although there is more variability in the way financial resources is measured, the most common variable is income. When household income or migrant earnings is included in the analysis, it is always

Table 5-3: Summary of Measures of Income Used by Various Studies in the Remittance Literature

Author(s)	Income	Significance of Income Variables
Banerjee (1984)	Monthly earnings of urban household plus quadratic term	Tobit: Income (+) and income-squared (-) significant. Probit: Income (+) and income-squared (-) significant. OLS: Income (+) and income-squared (-) significant.
Brown (1997, 1998)	Household income for twelve months prior to survey	Tobit: Income (+) significant.
Funkhouser (1995)	Whether or not the migrant household member is working overseas	*Salvadoran households:* Tobit: Significant (+). Probit: Significant (+). OLS: Significant (+). *Nicaraguan households:* Tobit: Significant (+). Probit: Significant (+). OLS: Not significant
Hoddinott (1982)	Migrant's monthly earnings	Tobit: Earnings (+) significant. Probit: Earnings (+) significant. OLS: Earnings (+) significant
Johnson and Whitelaw (1974)	Migrant's monthly income, plus quadratic and cube terms	OLS: Income (-), income squared (+) and income cubed (-) positive.
Knowles and Anker (1981)	Annual household income at migrant's current residence; annual income of household members residing away from migrant's residence	*Current residence:* Logistic: Income (+) and income-squared (-) significant. OLS: Income (+) and income-squared (-) significant.

Table 5-3: Summary of Measures of Income Used by Various Studies in the Remittance Literature *(Continued)*

Author(s)	Income	Significance of Income Variables
		Household members residing elsewhere: Logistic: Income and income-squared not significant. OLS: Income not significant.
Menjivar et al. (1998)	Income of all family members who live in household (logged)	Logistic: Income (+) significant. OLS: Income (+) significant

Note: Signs in parentheses in column 3 indicate sign of regression coefficient.

significant, as is shown in table 5-3. This clearly demonstrates the influence that income has on both the probability of remitting and the amount remitted. The other measures of financial resources used in the literature, such as household assets or the educational attainment of the migrant respondent, do not demonstrate this same pattern of consistency. One exception may be current employment status, which has a positive influence on remittance behavior (Funkhouser 1995; Menjivar et al. 1998). However, because of the high correlation between employment status and income, the significance of the employment status variables simply reflects the power of income (in the case of employment status, the presence or absence of income) on remittance behavior.

Accounting for Household Needs

In addition to accounting for the availability of financial resources for remitting, most studies on remittances also incorporate measures of resource need. These normally consist of variables accounting for the presence or absence in the household of the main migrant respondents' spouse, children, or other relatives (Banerjee 1984; Johnson and Whitelaw 1974; Knowles and Anker 1981; Menjivar et al. 1998). Other measures, such as household size (Brown 1998) or the dependency ratio of workers to non-workers in the household (Banerjee 1984), have been used as well. By incorporating these measures of need with income variables into the statistical analyses, these studies attempt to account for both the "supply" of available resources as well as the "demand" for those resources by household members.

A number of studies also consider the demands on household resources by family members living away from the main migrant respondent, either in the area or country of origin. Special attention has been paid to the presence or absence of those familial relationships, such as a spouse, child, parent, or sibling, in the area of origin that could positively influence remittance behavior (Banerjee 1984; Brown

1998; Johnson and Whitelaw 1974; Knowles and Anker 1981; Menjivar et al. 1998). Generally speaking, both the presence and absence of various family members significantly influences remittance behavior. The presence of the migrants' wives, children, and other close relatives in the household has been found to negatively influence both the probability of remitting and the amount remitted, while the presence of these same relatives in the area or country of origin has the opposite effect.

Adult Equivalent Income

As discussed above, most studies on remittance behavior include separate measures of income and household needs. In this research, to reduce the number of separate variables included in my analyses, measures of both income and needs are incorporated into a single adult equivalent income variable. Adult equivalence scales measure differences in the needs or requirements of households of different demographic composition. They do this by adjusting household income for both household size (i.e., number of people) and composition (i.e., number of adults vs. children, dual couple vs. single parent) and converting it to a form of per capita income, specifically, a per adult equivalent income. Equivalency scales also account for economies of scale. The second and subsequent persons in the household are given a lower weight than the first, under the assumption that many of the fixed household costs are accounted for by the first person and the incomes of the second and subsequent persons need not account for such costs (Myles 1996; Wolfson and Evans 1992; Burkhauser and Smeeding 1996). I use the "central variant scale" proposed by Wolfson and Evans (1992:46-47). The first adult in the household over the age of 18 is assigned a weight of 1.0. Each additional adult is given a weight of 0.4. The first and each subsequent child is given a weight of 0.3, except in the case of single parent households, where the first child is given a weight of 0.4 and each additional child is given a weight of 0.3. The weights for each household are totaled and divided into the household income, giving the adult equivalent income.

Adult equivalent income is also more advantageous than multiple measures of income and need in the analyses of remittance duration because of its lower correlation with the passage of time. One of the reasons why few studies have found that remittance duration significantly influences remittance behavior may be because the more conventional measures of income and need act as indirect measures of time. For example, household income may act as an indirect measure of time. Obviously, the longer the household has been settled overseas, the longer the period of integration. A longer settlement period usually translates into higher income. Because of this positive association, household income could indirectly reflect the passage of time.

Household size could also act as an indirect measure of time. This would be true if the variable were either a single measure of the number of persons in the household or several measures accounting for the presence or absence of a series of relatives. This could occur in two ways. First, as the process of chain migration continues and households receive new migrant members through time, the size of the household increases. Second, as migrant households become increasingly integrated into the country of destination, they could increase in size through both marriage and childbearing. In this way, it is probable that, on average, larger households have been overseas longer than smaller households. By including several of these measures that act as indirect measures of time, together these variables may control for enough of the time variance to make the remittance duration variables insignificant. Thus, in order to minimize the amount of time variance explained by the income and need variables, household income, size, and composition are collapsed into a single adult equivalent measure. The influence of indirect measures of time on the significance of the remittance duration variables is further discussed in the conclusion of this chapter.

MEASURES AND ANALYTICAL METHODS

Dependent Variables

Table 5-4 repeats the descriptive statistics for the baseline model explanatory variables, including the time overseas of the earliest migrant and the adult equivalent income,[xxii] for the FSM households in both Guam and Hawaii (see table 3-3). The earliest migrants in the Guam FSM households have been overseas about one and a half years longer than the earliest migrants in the Hawaii households. Also, Guam households have approximately $6,400 of income per adult equivalent, which is less than the $9,000 of the Hawaii households. Both the means are statistically different, reflecting the differences between the two migrant communities.

Table 5-4: **Descriptive Statistics for the Baseline Model Explanatory Variables, Guam and Hawaii, 1997**

Explanatory Variable	Guam (N=1,078)		Hawaii (N=791)	
	Mean	**SD**	**Mean**	**SD**
Remittance Duration				
Years Overseas, Earliest Migrant(a)	7.67	4.00	6.24	5.36
Household Financial Resources				
Adult Equivalent Income per $1,000(a)	6.44	7.65	9.03	21.97

Note: Each mean is based on a sub-sample of cases without missing values.
(a) Guam and Hawaii significantly different p<.001.

Curve Fitting Remittance Duration

According to the remittance decay hypothesis, the amount of money remitted overseas is low during the immediate post-migration period. As the migrant adjusts, remittances begin to increase, peaking soon after arrival. The amount remitted then begins to decline, eventually ceasing altogether. This suggests that the functional form between time and remittances is a quadratic equation (see chapter 2, figure 2-1). The remittance decay hypothesis is an individual level theory, but if this pattern of increase, peak, and decline holds at the household level, both the remittance duration variable and its square should be significant in the statistical models. Specifically, the linear term should be significant and positive, while the quadratic term should be significant and negative. In this research, both remittance duration and its square are included in the analyses to allow for a non-linear relationship between time and remittance behavior.

To determine if a quadratic equation adequately reflected the pattern in the remittance data, I divided the years overseas of the earliest migrant into five five-year time categories (i.e., 0-4, 5-9, 10-14, 15-19, and over 20 years) and analyzed the slopes of both the logistic and OLS regression analyses using a piecewise spline function (Schmertmann 1995). The plots suggest that a quadratic function adequately reflect the relationship between time and remittance behavior. This is especially true of the probability of remitting. In both Guam and Hawaii, the probability of remitting clearly increases, peaks, and declines through time. This pattern is less clear for the amount remitted, especially for Hawaii, but the plot of the slope does suggest a general pattern of remittance increase and decline through time.

RESULTS OF THE STATISTICAL ANALYSES

Time, Resources, and the Probability of Remitting

Table 5-5 (column 1) shows the results of the logistic regression analysis on the likelihood (log odds) of remitting, controlling for adult equivalent income. In both Guam and Hawaii, the likelihood of remitting is significantly influenced by both time and resources. In both equations, the years overseas of the earliest migrant and its square are significant and show that, through time, the likelihood of remitting rises, peaks, and declines. The slope of the quadratic equation indicates

Table 5-5:   **Multivariate Analysis of Duration on the Likelihood (Log Odds) of Remitting and Amount Remitted (Logged) with Controls for Adult Equivalent Income, Guam and Hawaii, 1997**

Explanatory Variable	Likelihood of Remitting (logistic regression) (1)	Amount Remitted (OLS regression) (2)
Guam	N=1,078	N=403
Intercept	-1.713 ***	4.818 ***
Remittance Duration		
Years Overseas, Earliest Migrant	0.119 **	0.076 **
Years Overseas, Earliest Migrant, Squared	-0.005 **	-0.004 **
Household Resources		
Adult Equivalent Income	0.138 ***	0.078 ***
Adult Equivalent Income, Squared	-0.294 ***	-0.111 **
Log Likelihood/R-squared	1,344.7	0.113
Hawaii	N=791	N=302
Intercept	-1.648 ***	5.666 ***
Remittance Duration		
Years Overseas, Earliest Migrant	0.155 ***	-0.007
Years Overseas, Earliest Migrant, Squared	-0.008 ***	0.001
Household Resources		
Adult Equivalent Income	0.101 ***	0.028 **
Adult Equivalent Income, Squared	-0.082 ***	-0.023 **
Log Likelihood/R-squared	938.9	0.023

Note: Adult equivalent income and square are per $1,000. The non-transformed values of the linear and squared coefficients are as follows: for the Guam logistic equation, 0.000138 and −2.94E-9; for the Hawaii logistic equation, 0.000101 and −8.15E-10; for the Guam OLS equation, 0.000078417 and −1.110529E-9; and for the Hawaii OLS equation, 0.000028255 and −2.33775E-10.
*Significant at p<.10. ** Significant at p<.05. ***Significant at p<.01.

that the likelihood of remitting continues to increase until 12 years in Guam and 10 years in Hawaii, then begins to decline.[xxiii]

Also in the Guam and Hawaii equations, the adult equivalent income variables are significant, indicating a positive association between household resources and the likelihood of remitting. As the per adult equivalent income increases, the amount of household discretionary income also increases, which increases the probability that the household will remit. The square of adult equivalent income is also significant, indicating that the likelihood of remitting declines at higher income levels. The slope of the equation indicates that the likelihood of remitting continues to increase until the adult equivalent income reaches $23,500 in Guam and $62,000 in Hawaii, then begins to decline. However, over 98 percent of the households in both Guam and Hawaii have adult equivalent incomes less than these peak values, so for the majority of FSM households, there is a positive, linear relationship between resources and the probability of remitting.

The influence of time on remittance behavior is best seen graphically. Figure 5-2 illustrates the additive effect of time on the predicated probability of remitting, holding adult equivalent income constant at the 25th, 50th, and 75th percentiles. It graphs the years overseas of the earliest migrant (from zero to twenty years) against the predicted probabilities derived from the baseline logistic regression coefficients presented in table 5-5. In both communities and at all three income levels, the predicted probability of remitting increases, peaks and declines through time.

Time, Resources, and the Amount Remitted

Table 5-5 (column 2) also shows the results of the OLS regression analysis on the log of the amount remitted, controlling for adult equivalent income. Only in Guam is the amount remitted significantly influenced by the passage of time. In the Guam equation, both the linear and quadratic terms are significant, indicating the amount remitted rises, peaks, and declines through time. The slope of the

Figure 5-2:   **The Additive Effect of Time on the Predicted Probability of Remitting, Holding Adult Equivalent Income Constant at the 25th, 50th, and 75th Income Percentiles, Guam and Hawaii, 1997**

GUAM

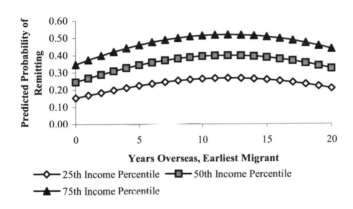

HAWAII

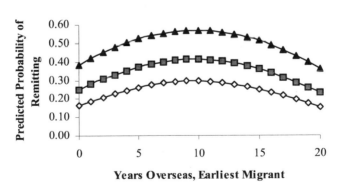

quadratic equation indicates that the amount remitted peaks at about 9.5 years then begins to decline. Neither remittance duration variables are significant in the Hawaii equation. The model for Hawaii was also run using only a linear functional form of remittance duration (not shown), but it was also found to be insignificant.

Unlike the duration variables, the adult equivalent income variables are significant in both the Guam and Hawaii OLS regression equations, indicating a positive association between household resources and the amount remitted. The slope of the equation indicates that the amount remitted continues to increase until the adult equivalent income reaches $35,000 for Guam and $60,000 for Hawaii. Considering that less than 2 percent of the households in both Guam and Hawaii have adult equivalent incomes higher than these peak values the association between available resources and the amount remitted is essentially positive and linear for the majority of FSM households.

Figure 5-3 illustrates the additive effect of time on the predicted amount remitted, holding adult equivalent income constant at the 25th, 50th, and 75th percentiles. It graphs the years overseas of the earliest migrant (from zero to twenty years) against the predicted amount remitted derived from the baseline OLS regression coefficients presented in table 5-5. The graph shows that the amount remitted by Guam households increases, peaks, and declines through time. In contrast, the slope of the amount remitted by Hawaii households is flat indicating an insignificant relationship between time and the amount remitted

CONCLUSION

The results of the baseline logistic and OLS regression analyses for both Guam and Hawaii show that, when time is measured at the household rather than the individual level, the likelihood (log odds) of remitting and the amount remitted rises, peaks, and declines through time. These initial results lend support to the ,remittance decay

Figure 5-3:   The Additive Effect of Time on the Predicted Amount Remitted, Holding Adult Equivalent Income Constant at the 25th, 50th, and 75th Income Percentiles, Guam and Hawaii, 1997

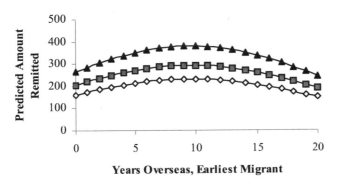

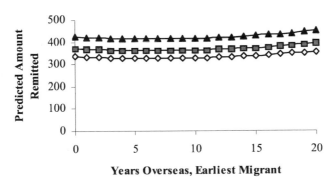

hypothesis. One of the reasons why studies have not more consistently found a significant influence of time on remittance behavior may be because researchers traditionally model a household behavior at the level of the individual. The comparison of regression models using both household and householder time, shown in table 5-2, provided an initial indication that the years overseas of the earliest migrant, rather than of a random migrant in the household, is a better measure of remittance duration. The results of additional statistical analyses (not shown) also support this view. To compare to the results of the baseline models using the years overseas of the earliest migrant, I ran the same analyses using the years overseas of the householder. In these equations, the time overseas of the householder and its quadratic term were significant only in the Hawaii logistic regression equation. As is shown in table 5-5, when the years overseas of the earliest migrant is used to represent time in the baseline model, the remittance duration variables are significant in both the Guam and Hawaii logistic and the Guam OLS regression equations.

These results suggest that while in certain circumstances either an individual or household measure of remittance duration will produce comparable results, the Guam analyses demonstrate that this is not always the case. Specifically, in older, more established migrant communities where households are more likely to be larger and are more likely to have experienced a higher level of continued in-migration of members, using the years overseas of the earliest migrant is a better measure of household remittance duration. This is because the years overseas of the earliest migrant ensures that the measure of remittance duration reflects the maximum number of years that the migrant household has been established in the country of destination. If the years overseas of a migrant other than the earliest migrant is used to measure time, or if the migrant is chosen randomly from all migrants in the household, it will on average cut time short. By systematically reducing the length of time overseas, in some circumstances individual-level measures of remittance duration can decrease the likelihood that time will be found to have a statistically significant influence over remittance behavior. However, in newly established communities where the households are small and have experienced little continued in-migration, there is a higher likelihood that a migrant randomly chosen to measure remittance duration is either the earliest migrant in the household or has been overseas for about the same amount of time. Under these circumstances, the difference between household and individual time is reduced and an individual measure of remittance duration can accurately reflect household time. This is because the individual level measure of duration adequately reflects the household measure of time, not the other way around. Using the time overseas of the earliest migrant is not only a better theoretical measure of remittance duration, but empirically as well.

The results of the baseline analyses also support the view that, in some cases, the income and needs variables used in other studies act as indirect measures of time and reduce the significance of the remittance duration variables. To compare to the results of the baseline models using adult equivalent income, I ran additional logistic and OLS regression analyses (not shown) using household income and household size, two variables that theoretically could act as indirect measures of time. These alternative models included five variables: time overseas of the earliest migrant and its square, household income and its square, and household size. In these equations, the remittance duration variables were significant only in the Hawaii logistic regression analysis. In the models controlling for adult equivalent income rather than household income and size (see table 5-5) the remittance duration variables are significant in both the Guam and Hawaii logistic and the Guam OLS regression equations. Admittedly, controlling for household income and size is not identical to controlling for adult equivalent income. However, these variables account for the influence of similar household characteristics, so these results suggest that the influence of time on remittance behavior is being mediated through the household income and size variables. Thus, while other empirical studies have failed to find statistically significant remittance duration variables, it does not necessarily mean that time has no effect on remittance behavior. Rather, remittance duration may be being accounted for by those variables such as household income and size that indirectly reflect the passage of time. Because income and needs variables are so commonly used in remittance research, this may help explain why studies have not more consistently found a significant influence of time on remittance behavior.

By modeling remittance duration at the household level, the results of the baseline analyses presented in this chapter show that both the probability of remitting and the amount remitted exhibit a pattern of quadratic decay, indicating that household remittance behavior increases, peaks, and declines through time. While these results support the remittance decay hypothesis, they provide little insight into the underlying social processes that would cause household remittance behavior to exhibit this particular pattern of decline. Chapter six focuses on explaining *why* household remittance behavior decays through time. As I will show, the pattern of household remittance decay is largely determined by continued migration, especially the processes of family reunification and household reconstitution overseas.

CHAPTER 6

The Influence of the Migration Process on Remittance Behavior

While the results of research in the literature provide little support for the remittance decay hypothesis, the results of the baseline analyses presented in chapter five show that when remittance duration is measured at the household level, both the probability of remitting and the amount remitted rise then decline through time. This lends support to the remittance decay hypothesis as formulated by Stark (1978). While the baseline analyses show that remittances increase then decline through time, they provide little insight into why household remittance behavior would exhibit this particular pattern of quadratic decay. That is, the results do not explain why the probability of remitting and the amount remitted rise and decline through time. Is this quadratic pattern of decay simply the result of mathematical curve fitting or does it reflect an underlying social process associated with remittance behavior?

In this chapter, I argue that the migration process, specifically family reunification migration, is the underlying social process that determines the remittance behavior of migrant households through time. Combined with the results of qualitative research on remittance behavior in Pacific migrant populations, the results presented in this chapter suggest a possible reason why remittance behavior exhibits a pattern of increase and decay. Remittance levels increase through time as the migrant household works to support dependent family members in the country of origin and to assist in their eventual migration. As the process of family reunification is gradually completed, fewer and fewer immediate kin remain overseas and remittance levels begin to decline. When the last migrant joins the household and all of the dependent family members have joined the earliest migrant overseas, the flow of remittances sent back home ends. The influence of the migration process not only explains why remittances decline, but why they continue through time. Households will continue remitting as long as their migrant members have dependent relatives overseas.

This chapter has three objectives. First, I discuss the hypothetical influence that the migration process has on household remittance behavior. I begin by dividing "household" time into two periods of "social" time that reflect the two stages of the household reunification process. These include 1) the time between the arrival of the first and last migrants, when the household is actively receiving new migrants and 2) the time after the arrival of the last migrant, when the process of family reunification has been completed. I hypothesize that for households reconstituting overseas through family reunification migration, the highest period of remittance activity should be between the arrival times of the first and last migrants when the households is receiving new members. The time after the arrival of the last migrant should be the lowest period of remittance activity.

Second, the influence of the migration process on remittance behavior is analyzed empirically by extending the baseline model presented in chapter five to include these two stages of household reunification. If the hypothetical positive relationship between family reunification migration and remittance behavior is true, then the time since the end of the family reunification process should be negatively associated with remittance behavior. That is, the longer period of time since the last migrant arrived, the higher the probability the household has completed the family reunification process and the lower the probability that the household will still be remitting. After controlling for the time since the arrival of the last migrant, the results demonstrate a negative association between the number of years since the arrival of the last migrant and the probability of remitting. This supports the posited relationship between family reunification and remittance behavior. It also supports the view that continued migration is the social process underlying remittance decay.

Third, the influence of continued and family reunification migration on household remittance behavior is examined. If it is true that households with dependent relatives overseas will continue remitting through time, then indicators of continued and family reunification migration should be positively associated with the probability of remitting. The results show that, in some cases, a positive association does exist. I also argue that time, in the form of remittance duration and decay, is more significant for those households reconstituting overseas. Continued and family reunification migration, by reflecting the temporal structure of the migration process, act as indirect measures of the passage of time. This suggests that the passage of time is more significant for the remittance behavior of those households with a history of continued migration and family reunification. This, in turn, suggests that the migration process is more important in explaining household remittance behavior than is the passage of time alone.

THE THEORETICAL INFLUENCE OF "SOCIAL TIME" ON REMITTANCE BEHAVIOR

In this section, I discuss the theoretical influence of the migration process on household remittance behavior. In order to understand why household remittance behavior changes through time, it is first necessary to understand how the migration process, which occurs over time, is filtered through the household context. Migrant households can be divided into two groups based on the type of migration that reestablished the household overseas. These include: 1) family migration, where all individuals in a household migrate at the same time, and 2) family reunification migration, where two or more individuals in the household migrate at different times. For households reestablished through family migration, the migration process ends with the simultaneous arrival of all household members overseas. This is not the case for households established through family reunification migration. In households where the migrant members arrive overseas at different times, the migration process does not end with the arrival of the first migrant. Rather, it ends when the last migrant arrives and the household is reconstituted overseas. In this sense, for many migrant households the migration process, as a social process, has a temporal structure. Time is not simply chronological time, but derives a social meaning from the migration process. I hypothesize that household remittance behavior, because it occurs within the context of the migration process, will reflect this temporal structure.

In chapter five, remittance duration was measured as the years overseas of the earliest migrant. I argued that this was a better indicator of remittance duration because it accounted for the entire length of time that the earliest migrant's household has been established overseas and, in this sense, is a better measure of "household time." For a migrant household, household time can be divided into two periods of "social time" that reflect the migration process (see figure 6-1). The first period is the time between the arrival of the earliest migrant and the last migrant to join the household. This is the period in time when the household is receiving migrants and is being reconstituted overseas. The second period is the time after the arrival of the last migrant when the household receives no more migrants.

Figure 6-1:   The Migration Process "Social Time" Line

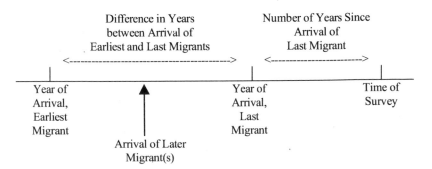

How are these two periods of "social time" reflected in household remittance behavior? As I argued in chapter 2 (see pp. 40-41), remittance decay only occurs in chain migrating households. This is because remittance decay reflects the gradual change and ending of those ties maintained by household members with immediate kin in the country of origin. Households will continue to remit as long as there are dependent family members in the country of origin. When the last migrant arrives and all dependent family members have joined the migrant household overseas, the flow of remittances sent back home ends. In this sense, remittance decay reflects family reunification migration and parallels the process of household reconstitution.

For chain migrating households, the most active period of remittance behavior will be the period of time between the arrival of the earliest and last migrants, when the household is reconstituting overseas. The level of remittance activity in this period will vary depending on where the household is in the family reunification process. Newly established households just beginning the process of reconstitution are likely to be less financially stable and therefore less able to remit, even though their motivation to remit is high. By comparison, older, more established households in the middle of the family reunification process are likely to have greater discretionary incomes and will be more likely to remit and remit at higher levels. Older, well-established households at the later stages of family reunification will be less likely to remit and will remit at lower levels when compared to households in the middle of the reconstitution process. As households complete the family reunification process and fewer dependent family members remain overseas, the motivation to remit declines. This decline is reflected in both the probability of remitting and the amount remitted during the later stages of household reconstitution.

While the most active period of remittance behavior is when the migrant household is receiving new members, the least active period will be the time after the arrival of the last migrant when family reunification has been completed. However, households established through family migration, where all immediate kin migrate at the same

time, do not experience family reunification migration and therefore do
not exhibit an active period of remittance behavior. For these
households, family reunification and household reconstitution is
completed with the simultaneous arrival of all household members
overseas. Households established through family migration do not
experience both periods of "social time" but only the period after
family reunification has been completed. Because all of the immediate
kin migrated together, no dependent family members remain back
home, and these households should therefore exhibit insignificant
levels of remittance behavior. I hypothesize that households
reconstituting overseas through a process of chain migration will be
more likely to remit and will remit at higher levels than will households
whose members migrated at the same time.

MEASURES AND ANALYTICAL METHODS

This section describes the explanatory variables used in the empirical
analyses. Table 6-1 repeats the means of the explanatory variables
included in the analyses, separately for the Guam and Hawaii Federated
States of Micronesia (FSM) migrant communities, and shows whether
the differences between the two groups are statistically significant (see
table 3-3). As table 6-1 indicates the two communities differ
considerably, and often significantly, in these characteristics.

Remittance Duration, or "Social Time"

In this analysis, two variables are used to measure the influence of time
and the migration process on household remittance behavior. These
variables reflect the two periods of "social time" illustrated in figure 6-
1. The first is the age of the household, measured by the years overseas
of the earliest migrant. The square of the years overseas of the earliest
migrant is also included to allow the effect of time on remittance
behavior to be non-linear. Like the analysis of remittance duration in
chapter five, a quadratic relationship between time and remittance

Table 6-1: Descriptive Statistics for the Explanatory Variables, Guam and Hawaii, 1997

Explanatory Variable	Guam (N=1,078)		Hawaii (N=791)	
	Mean	SD	Mean	SD
Remittance Duration				
Years Overseas, Earliest Migrant(c)	7.67	4.00	6.24	5.36
Years Since Arrival of Last Migrant	2.98	3.02	2.93	3.99
Household Financial Resources				
Adult Equivalent Income per $1,000(c)	6.44	7.65	9.03	21.97
Number of Adult and Proportion of Working Migrants				
Number of Migrants Age 16 and over(c)	3.94	2.37	2.41	1.64
Proportion of Migrants Age 16 and Over in the Labor Force(b)	58.67	35.49	54.21	41.76
Continued Migration				
Number of Migrant Groups or "Waves" Arriving after the Earliest Migrant(c)	1.04	1.30	0.55	0.91
Family Reunification(a)				
Earliest Migrant and All Relatives in Household Migrated in the Same Year(c)	0.14		0.09	
Earliest Migrant and One or More Relatives in Household Migrated in Different Years(c)	0.80		0.48	
Single Migrant in Household, Alone or with Non-relatives(c)	0.06		0.43	

Note: Each mean is based on a sub-sample of cases without missing values.
(a) Dummy variable
(b) Guam and Hawaii significantly different at p<.05.
(c) Guam and Hawaii significantly different at p<.001.

behavior exists if both the years overseas of the earliest migrant and its square are significant.

The second time variable is the years since the arrival of the last migrant in the household, which measures the number of years between the arrival of the last migrant and the year of the Micronesian Census. This variable controls for the influence of the length of time since the household received a new migrant member and is a proxy for the end of the family reunification process. Because the Micronesian Census is a cross-sectional survey, there is no way of knowing if the latest arrival is actually the last migrant or if the family reunification process is complete. Thus, I interpret the years since the arrival of the last migrant as a probability and hypothesize a negative association between this period of time and household remittance behavior. That is, the longer the period of time since the last migrant arrived, the higher the probability the household has completed the family reunification process and will receive no more migrants.

This interpretation is illustrated in figure 6-2. Households 1 through 4 have been established overseas for the same period of time. However, households 1 through 3 exhibit different periods of time since the last migrant joined the household. For household 1, the number of years since the arrival of the last migrant is low. Because this household has a history of family reunification, as indicated by the presence of a last migrant, and because the period of time since the last migrant arrived is short, the likelihood that this household is still in the process of reconstituting is high. Because it is likely that this household is currently experiencing family reunification migration, it is also likely to be actively remitting. For household 2, the years since the arrival of the last migrant is longer than that exhibited by household 1. This longer period of time may indicate that household 2 is farther along family reunification process than household 1. Because household 2 is more likely to have completed the reconstitution process, it is also less likely to remit than household 1. Compared to households 1 and 2, household 3 is the least likely to remit. This is because the number of years since the arrival of the last migrant is high. This may indicate that

Figure 6-2: **The Influence of the Years Since the Arrival of the Last Migrant on Household Remittance Behavior**

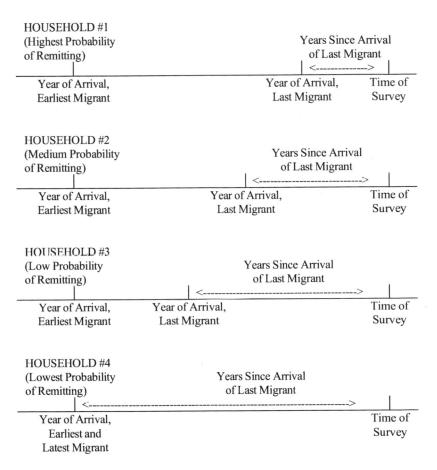

household 3 has already completed the family reunification process and is no longer remitting. Household 4 is the only household that did not experience any continued migration. Because it lacks a history of family reunification and has a high number of years overseas, household 4 is the least likely of all households to remit.

Household 4 is an example where the earliest migrant is both the first and last migrant. In these cases, the time since the arrival of the last migrant equals the years overseas of the earliest migrant. This implies that all migrants in the household arrived at the same time as the earliest migrant (i.e., family migration). In this research, if all migrants in the household arrived in the same year as the earliest migrant, then the value for the years overseas of the earliest migrant and its square are zero. Only the time since the arrival of the last migrant is used to measure remittance duration. A household with a single migrant (or a migrant living alone) is another example where the migrant is both first and last. In these cases, the years overseas of the earliest migrant and its square are set to zero, and the years since the arrival of the last migrant is used to measure remittance duration.

As can be seen in table 6-1, the years overseas of the earliest migrant and the time since last migrant arrival are longer in Guam than Hawaii, reflecting the older age of the migration flow to Guam. However, only the means of the years overseas of the earliest migrant are significantly different between the two communities. This means that while Guam households have had a longer period in which to receive new members, the households in both communities, on average, received their last migrant member at about the same time, approximately three years before the survey.

Continued Migration and Family Reunification

In this analysis, I include a variable that measures the level of continued migration experienced by the FSM migrant households. This variable measures the number of years new migrants have joined the household after the arrival of the earliest migrant. For example, if the earliest migrant in the household arrived in 1990, and one or more migrants arrived in the years 1994 and 1997, the household would have experienced two years (or "waves") of continued migration. The number of years new migrants joined the households *does not* measure the number of *individual migrants*. Instead, it measures the number of *migrant groups* that have joined the household through time. I use the number of "waves" rather than the number of migrants to account for the intensity of the migration process. In this research, I hypothesize that households reconstituted through a process of family reunification migration are more likely to remit than are households whose members migrated at the same time. Thus, households joined by one or more migrant groups will have a higher probability of remitting than will those households that have experienced no additional migration.

However, whether or not there is a positive relationship between the number of migrant "waves" and the likelihood of remitting may depend on where the average household is in the family reunification process. For example, if the majority of households in a migrant community are in the early-to-mid stages of family reunification, when a large number of kin remain in the country of origin, the number of migrant "waves" may be, on average, low but positively associated with the probability of remitting. Conversely, if the majority of households are in the mid-to-late stages, when few family members remain back home, the number of migrant "waves" may be, on average, high but negatively associated with the probability of remitting. Based on the migration history presented in chapter four, the characteristics of the Guam migrant households suggest they are, on average, actively reconstituting and in the middle of the reunification process. This means that, for the Guam migrant community, the association between migrant "waves" and the probability of remitting is likely to be positive. The migration stream to Hawaii is younger than the flow to Guam, with a large portion of newly established households that have experienced little continued migration. This suggests that the Hawaii migrants may be in the very early stages of the family reunification process, when households are not sufficiently established to remit. This may mean the number of migrant "waves" will not significantly influence the likelihood of remitting in Hawaii.

As can be seen in table 6-1, Guam households are twice as likely to receive an additional group of migrants than are Hawaii households. They also receive a higher number of migrants per "wave." Migrant groups joining Guam households' average 1.7 persons compared to 1.4 persons in the Hawaii migrant groups.

My measure of family reunification is a dummy variable that divides all households into three categories. The first category consists of family households that have experienced no family reunification, or those households in which the earliest migrant and all his/her relatives arrived in the same year. The second category consists of family households that have experienced family reunification, or those households in which one or more relatives of the earliest migrant arrived in years after the earliest migrant. The third category consists of non-family households where the earliest migrant either lives alone or with non-relatives. The reference category consists of those households where related migrants arrived in different years. As can be seen in table 6-1, the majority of households in both Guam (80 percent) and Hawaii (48 percent) have experienced family reunification. Only a small percent of households in both communities (14 percent in Guam and 9 percent in Hawaii) have experienced no family reunification. A much larger proportion of Hawaii households (43 percent) than Guam households (6 percent) consists of single migrants living alone or with non-relatives. All of these differences are statistically significant.

Household Financial Resources

The key measure of the influence of financial resources on remittance behavior is adult equivalent income. This measure was discussed in some detail in chapter five (see pp. 115-116). Both the adult equivalent income and its square are included in the models discussed in this chapter. Based on the results of the baseline model presented in chapter five, I hypothesize that adult equivalent income will be positively associated with both the probability of remitting and the amount remitted.

Number of Adult and Proportion of Working Migrants in Household

Two control variables, the number of adult migrants and the proportion of working migrants, are included in the analyses. Both of these measures could theoretically reinforce the household's propensity to remit. A higher number of adult migrants increases the likelihood that a larger pool of dependent family members remains in the country of origin, which would increase both the probability of remitting and the amount remitted. To control for any influence that the number of migrants has on household remittance behavior, the number of adult migrants age sixteen and over are included in the analyses. A second variable, the proportion of all adult migrants age 16 and over in the labor force, is included in the analysis to control for the influence that working migrants have on the household's ability to remit. Obviously, a high proportion of adult migrant laborers means few adult migrant dependents, which should increase the household's discretionary income. This would positively influence both the probability of remitting and the amount remitted.[xxiv]

As is shown in table 6-1, Hawaii households have a greater mean income than Guam households do. However, Guam households have a higher mean number of adults and a higher proportion of their adults in the labor force than do Hawaii households. These differences are statistically significant.

RESULTS

"Social Time" and Remittance Behavior

The results of the baseline model presented in chapter five (table 5-5) show that when remittance duration is measured at the household level, remittance behavior does exhibit a pattern of decay through time. When "social time" replaces "household time" in the baseline model, the results also demonstrate a pattern of remittance decay. This is especially true in the analysis of the households' probability of remitting. Table 6-2 shows the results of the multivariate analyses on the likelihood (log odds) of remitting and the amount remitted, controlling for adult equivalent income. The results of the logistic regression analyses (column 1) show that both the linear and quadratic time overseas of the earliest migrant variables for Guam and Hawaii are significant and indicate an inverse U-shaped relationship between time and the likelihood of remitting. The time since the arrival of last migrant also is significant in the Guam equation, indicating a negative association with time.

Because "social time" controls for the time since the arrival of the last migrant, the time overseas of the earliest migrant reflects the period of time between the arrival of the first and last migrant. The slopes of the quadratic equations indicate the households most likely to remit in Guam are those with eleven years between the arrival times of the first and last migrants and in Hawaii with nine years between the arrival times. Households with either smaller or larger differences in the arrival times are less likely to remit than these peak value households. This pattern of increase and decline in the likelihood of remitting again supports the remittance decay hypothesis as formulated by Stark (1978). The results are also consistent with the hypothesized relationship between the household's stage in the family reunification process and its probability of remitting. Households with small differences between the arrival times of the first and last migrants are likely to be in the early stages of settlement and household reconstitution and less likely to be able to remit. Households with a greater number of years between their arrival times will likely be better established and farther along the reunification process and will be the most likely of all households to remit. Households with large periods of time between their arrival times are likely to be at the end of the reunification process and comparatively less likely to remit.

The results are also consistent with the hypothesized relationship between the time since the arrival of the last migrant and the household's probability of remitting. In Guam, the time since the

Table 6-2:   **Multivariate Analysis of Duration on the Likelihood (Log Odds) of Remitting and Amount Remitted (Logged) with Controls for Adult Equivalent Income, Guam and Hawaii, 1997**

Explanatory Variable	Likelihood of Remitting (logistic regression) (1)	Amount Remitted (OLS regression) (2)
Guam	N=1,077	N=403
Intercept	-1.690 ***	4.823 ***
Remittance Duration		
Years Overseas, Earliest Migrant	0.159 ***	0.085 **
Years Overseas, Earliest Migrant, Squared	-0.006 ***	-0.004 **
Years Since Arrival of Last Migrant	-0.101 ***	-0.022
Household Resources		
Adult Equivalent Income	0.144 ***	0.079 ***
Adult Equivalent Income, Squared	-0.301 ***	-0.113 ***
Log Likelihood/R-Squared	1,326.4	0.116
Hawaii	N=784	N=302
Intercept	-1.636 ***	5.675 ***
Remittance Duration		
Years Overseas, Earliest Migrant	0.172 ***	0.004
Years Overseas, Earliest Migrant, Squared	-0.008 ***	0.001
Years Since Arrival of Last Migrant	-0.038	-0.037
Household Resources		
Adult Equivalent Income	0.101 ***	0.030 **
Adult Equivalent Income, Squared	-0.083 ***	-0.025 **
Log Likelihood/R-Squared	936.6	0.032

Note: Adult equivalent income and square are per $1,000. The non-transformed values of the linear and squared coefficients are as follows: for the Guam logistic equation, 0.000144 and –3.01E-9; for the Hawaii logistic equation, 0.000101 and –8.21E-10; for the Guam OLS equation, 0.00007924 and –1.134447E-9; and for the Hawaii OLS equation, 0.000030393 and –2.48558E-10.
*Significant at p<.10. **Significant at p<.05. ***Significant at p<.01.

arrival of the last migrant is significant and negative, suggesting the longer the period of time since the arrival of the last migrant, the less likely the household is to remit. The longer the period of time since the arrival of the last migrant, the more likely the household has completed the family reunification process, which would reduce the probability of remitting. The time since the arrival of the last migrant is also negative in the Hawaii equation, which is in the expected direction, but it is not significant.

In the Guam OLS analysis, only the years overseas of the earliest migrant and its square are significant (see table 6-2, column 2). Their significance indicates an inverse U-shaped relationship between time and the amount remitted. The slope of the quadratic equation indicates that households with nine years between the arrival of the first and last migrants remit the most. Households with either smaller or larger differences in arrival times are less likely to remit than these peak value households. As with the likelihood of remitting, the amount remitted by Guam households rises and declines through time, again supporting the remittance decay hypothesis. The results are also consistent with the hypothesized relationship between the households' stage in the family reunification process and the amount remitted. Older, more financially established households in the middle of the family reunification process remit more than either younger, less financially stable households or older households that have completed the reunification process. The time since the arrival of the last migrant is in the expected direction but is not significant.

None of the remittance duration variables are significant in the Hawaii OLS analysis, which is consistent with the results of the baseline OLS analysis. This suggests that time does not significantly influence the amount remitted by Hawaii migrant households.

Finding the inflection point

The results of the "social time" analyses show that remittances increase and decline through time. To see if either the arrival of a particular relative of the earliest migrant or the achievement of a particular family structure (e.g., nuclear family) is associated with the beginning of the decline, I ran additional logistic and OLS regression analyses (not shown). The presence or absence of the earliest migrant's spouse, children, parents, siblings, and other relatives were included in the analyses to determine if they have any influence on remittance duration. Several family structures were also analyzed, including the presence or absence of the earliest migrant's nuclear family, family of orientation, and extended family.[xxv]

The years between the arrival of the first and last migrants was divided into two periods measuring the time before and after either the arrival of the relative or the achievement of the particular family structure. For example, to determine the influence of the arrival of the spouse on remittance behavior, two time periods were included in the analysis: 1) the time before the arrival of the spouse, measured as the difference between the year of arrival of the earliest migrant and his/her spouse, and 2) the time between the arrival of the spouse and the last migrant. The time after the arrival of the last migrant was also included in the models.[xxvi] I hypothesized that if the relative or household structure was associated with the beginning of the decline in remittance behavior, then the pre-arrival period should be significant and positive and the post-arrival period should be significant and negative.

The results of these analyses suggest that no single relative and no particular household structure is associated with the beginning of the decline in either the probability of remitting or the amount remitted. In none of the Guam and Hawaii OLS and the Hawaii logistic regression analyses are any of the remittance duration variables significant. In the Guam logistic regression analyses, however, an interesting pattern appeared. In all of the regression equations, the pre-arrival period was significant and positive, the post-arrival period was insignificant, and the years since the last migrant arrival was significant and negative. This seems to suggest that, at least in the FSM households on Guam, the probability of remitting continues to increase as the relatives of the earliest migrant are joining the household overseas, but that after the arrival of the last migrant, the probability of remitting declines. This supports my hypothesis about the positive influence of continued migration on remittance behavior.

Continued Migration, Family Reunification, and the Probability of Remitting

Table 6-3 shows the results of the logistic regression analysis on the likelihood (log odds) of remitting for both Guam and Hawaii, controlling for social time, available resources, the number of adult and proportion of working migrants, and the processes of continued migration and family reunification.[xxvii] The results provide some support for the positive influence of continued migration on household remittance behavior. As I show in table 6-3, continued migration positively influences the likelihood of remitting in Guam. That is, for every group or "wave" of migrants that arrive after the earliest migrant, the probability of remitting for Guam households increases. This positive association suggests the Guam migrant households are in the early-to-middle stages of the family reunification process, when the migrant "waves" would be positively associated with increasing remittance activity. The results also show that, in Hawaii, the number of arriving migrant groups has no influence on household remittance behavior. This suggests the Hawaii migrant households are in the very early stages of family reunification, before active household reconstitution and remittance behavior has begun.

The results also provide support for a positive association between family reunification migration and household remittance behavior. In both Guam and Hawaii, households that were established through family reunification migration are more likely to remit than are households whose members migrated at the same time. However, only in the Guam equation is this difference statistically significant. Also in both Guam and Hawaii, single migrant households are significantly less likely to remit than are households that were established through family

Table 6-3:   **Multivariate Analysis of Duration on the Likelihood (Log Odds) of Remitting with Controls for Other Explanatory Variables, Guam and Hawaii, 1997**

Explanatory Variable	Likelihood of Remitting (logistic regression)	
	Guam N=1,077	Hawaii N=784
Intercept	-1.854***	-2.107***
Remittance Duration		
Years Overseas, Earliest Migrant	0.013	0.115**
Years Overseas, Earliest Migrant, Squared	-0.001	-0.006***
Years Since Arrival of Last Migrant	0.012	-0.015
Household Resources		
Adult Equivalent Income	0.098***	0.054***
Adult Equivalent Income, Squared	-0.204***	-0.038**
Number of Adult and Proportion of Working Migrants		
Number of Migrants Age 16 and Over	0.058	0.088
Proportion of Migrants Age 16 and Over in the Labor Force	0.009***	0.017***
Continued Migration		
Number of Migrant Groups or "Waves" Arriving after the Earliest Migrant	0.165**	-0.045
Family Reunification(a)		
Earliest Migrant and All Relatives in Household Migrated in the Same Year	-0.512**	-0.328
Single Migrant in Household, Alone or with Non-Relatives	-1.068***	-0.596**
Log Likelihood	1,288.5	872.6

Note: Adult equivalent income and square are per $1,000. The non-transformed values of the linear and squared coefficients are as follows: for the Guam logistic equation, 0.000098 and –2.04E-9; and for the Hawaii logistic equation, 0.000054 and –3.79E-10.
(a) Reference category: Earliest migrant and one or more relatives in household migrated in different years.
*Significant at p<.10. **Significant at p<.05. ***Significant at p<.01.

reunification migration. Of all household types, single migrant households are the least likely to remit.

The results of both the Guam and Hawaii analyses indicate that the number of adult migrants does not significantly influence whether or not the household remits. However, the proportion of adult migrants in the labor force does significantly influence the households' probability of remitting. In both the Guam and Hawaii equations, an increase in the proportion of migrants age 16 and over in the labor force positively influences the household's chance of remitting. These results suggest that the household's remittance probability is more influenced by the proportion of migrants in the labor force who generate income than by the number of migrants themselves.

Adult equivalent income remains a strong positive predictor of the probability of remitting for both Guam and Hawaii migrant households. Both the linear and quadratic terms remain statistically significant even after controlling for all other variables. These results underscore the fundamental importance of household resources in remittance behavior.

Although "social time" was found to positively influence the likelihood of remitting in Guam households (see table 6-2), once the number of migrant "waves" and family reunification variables are included in the analysis, remittance duration is no longer significant. Considering these two variables reflect both periods of "social time," especially the time between the arrival of the first and last migrant, it is not surprising their inclusion would reduce the significance of the duration coefficients. While the results of the Guam analysis initially suggest that the passage of time does not influence the probability that a household will remit, I would argue that this is not the case. Rather, "social time" is represented directly and indirectly through several variables included in the model. This suggests that time, far from being an insignificant influence in the probability of remitting, influences household remittance behavior indirectly, rather than directly, through the processes of continued migration and family reunification. In the Hawaii analysis, neither the number of migrant "waves" nor the family reunification variables are significant. However, the remittance duration variables remain significant.

Continued Migration, Family Reunification and the Amount Remitted

Table 6-4 shows the results of the OLS regression analysis on the log of the amount remitted for both Guam and Hawaii, controlling for social time, available resources, the number of adult and proportion of working migrants, and the processes of continued migration and family reunification.[xxviii] Compared to the logistic regression analyses of the likelihood of remitting, few variables in the OLS regression analyses significantly influence the amount remitted in either the Guam or Hawaii households. The number of migrant "waves" is not significant in either the Guam or Hawaii analyses, suggesting that the continued migration of new household members does not influence the amount remitted. In Guam, the level of family reunification also has no effect on the amount of money remitted by migrant households. In Hawaii, however, single migrant households are significantly less likely to remit than households that have experienced family reunification migration. This may reflect the high proportion of single migrant households in the Hawaii community, households that may be less able financially to remit.

The proportion of migrants in the labor force does not influence the amount remitted by either Guam or Hawaii households. However, in Guam households, the number of adult migrants does positively influence the amount remitted. With every additional adult migrant, the amount remitted by the household increases by approximately 6 percent. This positive association may reflect the larger pool of dependent family members a higher number of adult migrants would have in the country of origin. While a higher number of immediate kin back home does not increase the probability of remitting, as suggested by the results of the logistic regression analyses, it does increase the amount of money sent each time a household remits. The number of adult migrants does not significantly influence the amount remitted by Hawaii households.

Table 6-4:   **Multivariate Analysis of Duration on the Amount Remitted (Logged) with Controls for Other Explanatory Variables, Guam and Hawaii, 1997**

Explanatory Variable	Amount Remitted (OLS regression)	
	Guam N=403	Hawaii N=302
Intercept	4.641***	5.632***
Remittance Duration		
Years Overseas, Earliest Migrant	0.026	-0.033
Years Overseas, Earliest Migrant, Squared	-0.002	0.002
Years Since Arrival of Last Migrant	0.024	-0.010
Household Resources		
Adult Equivalent Income	0.064***	0.028**
Adult Equivalent Income, Squared	-0.081*	-0.218*
Number of Adult and Proportion of Working Migrants		
Number of Migrants Age 16 and Over	0.054**	0.049
Proportion of Migrants Age 16 and Over in the Labor Force	0.002	0.003
Continued Migration		
Number of Migrant Groups or "Waves" Arriving after the Earliest Migrant	0.055	-0.050
Family Reunification(a)		
Earliest Migrant and All Relatives in Household Migrated in the Same Year	-0.050	-0.096
Single Migrant in Household, Alone or with Non-Relatives	-0.327	-0.409*
R-squared	0.143	0.055

Note: Adult equivalent income and square are per $1,000. The non-transformed values of the linear and squared coefficients are as follows: for the Guam OLS equation, 0.000064172 and -8.10779E-10; and for the Hawaii OLS equation, 0.000027801 and -2.1758E-10.
(a) Reference category: Earliest migrant and one or more relatives in household migrated in different years.
*Significant at $p<.10$. **Significant at $p<.05$. ***Significant at $p<.01$.

The only variable to significantly influence the amount remitted in both Guam and Hawaii households is the adult equivalent income. The results indicate that, as expected, there is a positive association between adult equivalent income and the amount remitted. The change in adult equivalent income has a stronger influence on the amount remitted by Guam migrant households. In Guam, each 10 percent increase in adult equivalent income is associated with a 6.3 percent increase in the amount of money remitted. In Hawaii, each 10 percent increase is associated with a 2.8 percent increase in the amount remitted.

The remittance duration variables are insignificant in both the Guam and Hawaii OLS regression equations. "Social time" was found to significantly influence the amount remitted by Guam migrant households (see table 6-2), but once the control variables are included in the model, remittance duration is no longer significant. The only variable to consistently influence the amount remitted in both Guam and Hawaii is adult equivalent income. This suggests a household's financial resources have a greater influence on the amount remitted than does the mere passage of time. This interpretation receives some additional support from the Hawaii results. Single migrant households were found to remit significantly less money overseas than households established through family reunification migration. In Hawaii, single migrant households have lower average incomes than all other household types,[xxix] which suggests they have less discretionary income and a lower ability to remit money overseas.

SUMMARY AND CONCLUSION

The results presented in chapter five demonstrate that, when time is measured at the household rather than the individual level, remittances rise then decline through time. The likelihood of remitting in both Guam and Hawaii and the amount remitted in Guam clearly demonstrate a quadratic pattern of decay, indicating that household remittance behavior rises, peaks, and declines through time. What these results fail to tell us is *why* remittance behavior declines through time and why it would demonstrate this particular pattern of decay. Is the quadratic pattern of decay exhibited by the baseline regression analyses simply the result of mathematical curve fitting or does it reflect an underlying social process associated with remittance behavior?

The results of the "social time" baseline analyses presented in this chapter suggest that the migration process, specifically the process of household reconstitution overseas, is the underlying social process influencing the remittance behavior of migrant households. Using the baseline measures of "household time," I incorporated an additional control variable into "social time" measuring the time since the arrival of the last migrant to the household. This enabled me to analyze the influence of two time periods on remittance behavior: 1) the period of time between the arrival of the earliest and last migrant and 2) the time after the arrival of the last migrant. The results are consistent with the hypothesized quadratic association between the household's stage in the family reunification process and its remittance behavior. They are also consistent with the hypothesized negative association between the end of the family reunification process and remittance behavior. The results also support my main hypothesis that households established through family reunification migration are more likely to remit than households whose members migrated at the same time. However, a history of family reunification migration seems to have a greater influence on the household's probability of remitting than on the amount remitted.

The results of the "social time" baseline analyses suggest a reason why household remittance behavior exhibits a quadratic pattern of decay through time. Initially, one or a few members of a household emigrate from the country of origin, establishing an overseas "extension" of the household in the country of destination. As the migrant household establishes itself economically, both the probability of remitting and the amount remitted are initially low but increase as migrant household members work to support dependent members overseas and to assist in their eventual migration. As the process of household reconstitution is gradually completed, fewer and fewer dependents remain overseas and remittance levels peak and begin to decline. When the last migrant emigrates and all dependent family members have joined the migrant household overseas, the flow of remittances back home ends. This is not to say that all of the migrant household's dependent family members, either immediate or more distant kin, migrate and become part of the household overseas. Many of those kin may have established themselves economically in the country of origin, do not require financial assistance, and do not desire to migrate. Other kin may have migrated elsewhere, using other channels of assistance. Some kin may have died during the period of household reconstitution. All of these processes would further reduce the number of dependent relatives the migrant household has in the country of origin. This would reduce the amount of time needed to reestablish a household overseas, which would, in turn, reduce the period of active remittance behavior.

Support from the Literature

The qualitative literature on Pacific Island migrant communities provides numerous examples that indicate this is a plausible explanation of remittance decay. The use of "scout" migrants as a way to establish household extensions in countries overseas, with the express purpose of further family reunification migration, has been detailed by researchers studying Cook Island, Tongan, and Samoan migrant communities (Curson 1979; MacPherson 1994; Small 1997). Curson (1979:188-89) refers to this process as "delayed family migration," where a household member, usually the male household head, migrates from the Cook Islands to New Zealand and later sends for his wife, children, and possibly other relatives as well. This results in what Small (1997:7) refers to as a "transnational family." A number of studies have documented this early period of household reconstitution, which lasts between three to five years, as the highest period of remittance activity (Loomis 1990; MacPherson 1994; Vete 1995). These early migrants make great personal sacrifices, including foregoing household amenities such as telephones and washing machines and working second jobs to maximize their ability to remit

(Ahlburg 2000; James 1993; MacPherson 1994; Small 1997; Vete 1995). In some cases, the remittances sent home by these early migrants would be used to support their immediate family, their more distant kin, and various village projects as well (Curson 1979; James 1995; MacPherson 1994; Vete 1995).

After the early migrants achieve financial stability, many begin to facilitate the migration of their relatives, often by remitting air fare, offering free room and board, and arranging employment (Curson 1979; MacPherson 1994; Small 1997; Vete 1995). Research by MacPherson (1994) among Samoan migrants in New Zealand suggests three motives for sponsoring relatives. First, by sponsoring immediate kin, such as a sibling, the burden of supporting close relatives can be shared. Large projects, such as building a house for family members back home, can be achieved quicker with multiple income earners contributing remittances. Second, by sponsoring lateral kin, such as a cousin, the burden of supporting more distant relatives is shifted from the earliest migrant to the more immediate relatives of those distant kin. Third, by sponsoring immediate kin, such as spouses, children, and especially parents, the migrants have greater control over their expenditures. By reuniting all dependent family members under one roof overseas, resources previously used for remitting can be spent directly on the needs of immediate kin and not be diverted to pay for extra-familial or village-based expenses.

As the process of household reconstitution is completed and fewer dependent members remain in the country of origin, remittances begin to decline (Curson 1979; MacPherson 1994; Small 1997; Stanwix and Connell 1995; Vete 1995). Stanwix and Connell (1995) found that, among Fijian households in Australia, the highest remitters were those with dependent family members still in Fiji, while Vete (1995) found that remittances sent to Tonga by Tongan migrants declined as the number of dependents living in the New Zealand household increased. However, processes in addition to migration can change the ratio of country of origin to country of destination dependents. This includes the economic independence of family members back home. Among

Fijian migrants in Australia, good income and labor force participation of relatives in Fiji were given as reasons for sending low or no remittances (Stanwix and Connell 1995). The remittance burden of overseas households is also reduced when these economically stable households in the country of origin take responsibility for the care of mutual relatives, such as an elderly parent (MacPherson 1994; Small 1997). The migrant households' remittance burden is further reduced when dependent relatives use their own network contacts, such as those established through marriage, to migrate independently, often to countries other than that of the earliest migrant (MacPherson 1994; Small 1997). Death of elderly relatives can also reduce the number of dependents back home (MacPherson 1994; Small 1997). Through time, as the number of dependent kin declines, remittances also decline. An informant told MacPherson (1994:100) that she no longer remits much money to Samoa "because there's not many of my family still there." Eventually, as the number of dependent family members in the country of origin approaches zero, remittances end. Vete (1995:65) found that a common reason why Tongan migrants no longer remitted was "because none of us is in Tonga." The migrants' nuclear families, parents and siblings were all overseas and there was no reason to send money home, even if more distant kin, such as cousins, remained in Tonga.

Explaining Remittance Duration

The results of the "social time" baseline analyses and qualitative data provided by the literature on Pacific Island migrants suggests that the quadratic pattern of household remittance decay reflects the process of household reconstitution by migrants overseas. Both the probability of remitting and the amount remitted increase and peak while the earliest migrants are sponsoring the continued migration of their dependent relatives, and as this reunification process is completed, and few or no dependent relatives are left in the country of origin, the households cease remitting. The influence of family reunification migration not only helps explain why remittances decline but why they would continue through time as well. Households with dependent relatives in the country of origin will continue remitting until all of those relatives have either joined the earliest migrants overseas or until their dependence has been nullified (through economic independence, migration elsewhere, death, etc.).

This view of remittance duration received some support from the analyses presented in this chapter. If it is true that households with dependent relatives overseas will continue remitting through time, then households with a history of continued and family reunification migration should be more likely to remit than should households that have never received additional migrant family members. I use two indicators of continued and family reunification migration in my analyses. These include: 1) the number of "waves" or groups of migrant arrivals and 2) whether or not the earliest migrant and all relatives in the household arrived together or chain-migrated over a period of time. As the results of the Guam analyses show, both the number of migrant group arrivals and a history of family reunification migration were found to have a positive influence on the household's probability of remitting. The amount remitted appears to be more influenced by the household's financial ability to remit, not by its migration history, as indicated by both the Guam and Hawaii results.

Time Revisited

In both the Guam logistic and OLS regression analyses, once the effects of continued and family reunification history are controlled for statistically, the "social time" variables are no longer significant. From these results, it could easily be concluded that time has no effect on remittance behavior in Guam, either the likelihood of remitting or the amount remitted. However, because the number of migrant "waves" and the level of family reunification reflect the continued migration process, they act as *indirect* measures of the passage of time. That is, the influence of time on remittance behavior acts through the processes of household reconstitution and family reunification migration. This means that time is more significant for the remittance behavior of those households that are established through continued migration. This is because remittance duration ultimately reflects the temporal structure of the migration process. This suggests that the migration process is more important in explaining household remittance behavior than is the passage of time alone.

Recognizing the fundamental importance of the migration process on remittance behavior can help explain the divergent findings in the literature regarding the passage of time. If a migrant population is established through the process of family migration, where entire family units migrate overseas, it is probable that this population will exhibit low aggregate remittance levels and a short, statistically insignificant period of remittance activity. For example, Fiji Indian migration tends to be dominated by family units, which may help explain their reported low remittance rates (Raj 1991). However, if a migrant population is established through family reunification migration, the period of significant remittance behavior will reflect the average time it takes a migrant household to reconstitute overseas. Aggregate remittances will remain high as long as migrants continue to establish household extensions in the country of destination. This may help explain why the remittance levels of Cook Island, Samoan, and Tongan migrants in Australia and New Zealand have been found to remain high over an extended period of time (Curson 1979; James 1991; Loomis 1990; MacPherson 1994; Vete 1995). These migrant populations were initially established by "scout" migrants and quickly shifted to chain and household reconstitution migration, a process that continued into the 1990s and was galvanized by the family reunification policies of the New Zealand and Australian governments.

Recognizing the influence of the migration process on remittance behavior not only can help explain why remittances occur and continue through time but why previously high remittance levels decline and end. At the household level, remittances will decline and end as the migrant household completes the process of family reunification in the country of origin. At the aggregate level, remittances will decline and end as the number of household extensions established overseas also declines and ends. In other words, the maintenance of high aggregate remittance levels depends on the migrants' continued migration and the continued process of household reconstitution through time. The processes of migration and household reconstitution could end "naturally" if, for example, all of the migrants from a given country of origin who wanted to leave have already left. However, more realistically, these processes ultimately depend on the migration policies of the country of destination. This is especially significant for those small Pacific Island countries, such as Tonga, Samoa, and the Cook Islands, whose economies have become increasingly dependent on the inflow of remittances from overseas. As long as the migration policy of the dominant receiving countries, including Australia, New Zealand, and the United States, maintains a pro-family reunification orientation, Pacific Islanders will be able to migrate, establish household extensions and, on the aggregate level, continue to remit. Once the ability to migrate overseas is curtailed, aggregate remittance levels will decline and eventually end.

Conclusion

The results presented in this chapter support my hypothesis that continued migration and family reunification, as reflections of both household reconstitution and the migration process, have a positive influence on household remittance behavior. Support for this hypothesis comes primarily from the Guam analyses, especially the logistic regression results. In the Hawaii analyses, the continued migration variables were not significant in either the logistic or OLS equations. The differences between the Guam and Hawaii results probably are due to the differences in their population compositions, which reflect the age of the migration flows, as discussed in chapter four. A large proportion of FSM migrant households in Hawaii are newly established households that have probably not been overseas long enough to have experienced a high level of continued migration and have not had the time to fully reconstitute. Approximately 45 percent of all households in Hawaii have been overseas less than five years, with 26 percent established within the last two years. This is compared to Guam, where only 19 percent of all households have been overseas less than five years and only 8 percent established within the last two years. Also, Hawaii has a much higher proportion of single migrant households. Approximately 43 percent of all households in Hawaii are non-family households compared to only 6 percent in Guam. Of the single migrant households in Hawaii, 61 percent have been established less than five years, with 41 percent established within the last two years. Clearly, these statistics indicate that the FSM migrant population in Hawaii has had less time than the Guam population to complete the family reunification process and establish households overseas. The influence of the migration process on the remittance behavior of migrant households in Hawaii is insignificant because enough time has not passed to see its effect.

This chapter has focused on explaining why household remittance behavior exhibits a quadratic pattern of decay. As the results of the analysis have shown, the pattern of remittance decay is determined by continued migration, especially the processes of family reunification and household reconstitution overseas. In the next chapter, the analyses assess the impact of the influence of migrant network participation on household remittance behavior. The results show that remittance behavior is reinforced among households that maintain their ethnic links in the host society and their ties to the country of origin.

CHAPTER 7

Network Participation and Remittance Behavior

The goal of this research is to investigate the association between time and remittance behavior and to provide an explanation why, in some migrant communities, remittances rise then decline through time while in other communities remittances are maintained at high levels over long periods. Chapter five demonstrated that when remittance behavior was modeled at the household level, both the probability of remitting and the amount remitted increases, peaks, and declines through time. Chapter six took this analysis one step further by including a measure of "social" time into the model, which incorporated the influence of the migration process on remittance behavior. The results of the "social time" analyses show that a quadratic pattern of decay is exhibited by those households with a history of continued migration. Further analysis demonstrated that, in some cases, the migration history of the household, including the number of migrant "waves" and level of family reunification, has a positive influence on remittance behavior. These results suggest that the active period of remittance behavior is when the household is receiving new migrants and reconstituting overseas. Remittance behavior will continue as long as the household is receiving new migrants and will end when the migration process, in the form of household reconstitution and family reunification migration, also ends.

This chapter looks beyond the household and focuses on the influence that migrant social networks have on remittance behavior. Migrant network theory suggests that active and continual network participation by household members positively influences both the likelihood of remitting and the amount remitted. Network participation results in higher remittance behavior because it retards the migrants' adaptation to and assimilation into the host society. By encouraging migrants to maintain a high level of social ties with other co-ethnics and an orientation to the culture and society of origin, network participation also encourages migrants to maintain their relationships with non-migrants overseas and continue remitting. As I will show, the results presented in this chapter support a positive relationship between network participation and remittance behavior. They also provide support for the hypothetical link between the level of integration and network participation and their influence on remittance behavior.

This chapter focuses on the influence that the participation in migrant networks by household members has on household remittance behavior. I hypothesize that households whose members participate in migrant networks are more likely to remit and remit at higher levels than are those whose members have isolated themselves from migrant networks. By helping to maintain the relationship between migrants and non-migrants, network participation can help explain why in some migrant communities remittance behavior persists through time.

MEASURES AND ANALYTICAL METHODS

Table 7-1 repeats the means of the explanatory variables included in the analysis for the Guam and Hawaii Federated States of Micronesia (FSM) migrant communities and indicates whether the differences are statistically significant (see table 3-3). As table 7-1 shows, the two communities differ, and often significantly, in almost all of their characteristics. This section describes the explanatory variables used in the analysis.

Table 7-1: Descriptive Statistics for the Explanatory Variables, Guam and Hawaii, 1997

Explanatory Variable	Guam (N=1,078)		Hawaii (N=791)	
	Mean	SD	Mean	SD
Remittance Duration				
Years Overseas, Earliest Migrant(c)	7.67	4.00	6.24	5.36
Years Since Arrival of Last Migrant	2.98	3.02	2.93	3.99
Household Financial Resources				
Adult Equivalent Income per $1,000(c)	6.44	7.65	9.03	21.97
Network Participation				
Social Expenditures as a Percent of Total Household Income(b)	0.10	0.43	0.06	0.33
Percent of Non-Micronesians in Household(c)	0.02	0.10	0.07	0.20
Trips to the FSM (a)(c)	0.50		0.17	
Receipt of Remittances by Household from Overseas(a)(c)	0.02		0.13	
English Use in the Home:(a)(c)				
Other Exclusively or Other More Frequently than English	0.76		0.51	
Other and English Equally or Other Less Frequently than English	0.07		0.23	
English Exclusively	0.17		0.26	

Note: Each mean is based on a sub-sample of cases without missing values.
(a) Dummy variable.
(b) Guam and Hawaii significantly different at p<.01.
(c) Guam and Hawaii significantly different at p<.001.

Measuring Network Participation

The data sets available for analysis by migration specialists rarely, if ever, include variables reflecting migrant network participation. Like most data sets, the Census of Micronesian Migrants does not include any direct measures of network participation. Because of this, the analyses presented in this chapter only include *indirect* measures of household network participation.

What are some of the likely characteristics of households that participate in migrant networks? Research by Boyd (1989) on family and personal networks in international migration offers some clues. Boyd (1989:650-651) suggests four ways migrant networks are maintained by their members through time. These include: 1) return migration, which further links sending and receiving communities and facilitates the continued use of migrant networks; 2) visits to the country of origin by migrants who have settled in the receiving country, which renew the bonds between migrants and non-migrants; 2) reliance on social activities sponsored by the wider migrant community, such as sports associations or village celebrations, which encourages a continued orientation to the society of origin; and 4) marriages that sustain kinship obligations across time and space. Households whose members participate in migrant networks should exhibit these same characteristics.

The information provided by the Micronesian Census has allowed me to create two of the four indicators suggested by Boyd (1989). These include indicators of return trips to the sending country and a reliance on in-group social activities. Unfortunately, the Micronesian Census does not include questions asking about the return migration history of the household. Also, because the rate of marital endogamy is so high among the Micronesian migrants in both Guam and Hawaii, there are too few households with exogamously married couples to include in the analysis. Three additional measures of household network participation also are included. These are whether or not the household received remittances from overseas, the level of English use in the household, and the percent of non-Micronesians in the household. The following provides details about the variables used in this analysis.

Return trips to the FSM

Trips by migrants to their country of origin as well as visits by their friends and relatives from overseas should have a positive influence on remittance behavior because they renew and strengthen the ties between migrant and non-migrants. There is some evidence for this positive influence in the literature. In a study of remittance behavior among Tongans and Western Samoans in Australia, Brown (1998) found that visits from friends or relatives from the islands positively influenced the amount of remittances sent overseas. No study to date has analyzed the influence return trips home by household members has on remittance behavior. It seems logical that return trips home would have the same positive effect on remittance behavior as visits by friends or relatives from overseas. In this analysis, I include a dummy variable that measures whether or not anyone in the migrant household has taken a trip to the FSM in the last twelve months. By helping to maintain the relationship between migrants and non-migrants, a return trip home to the FSM should be positively associated with both the probability of remitting and the amount remitted.

As is shown in table 7-1, Guam households were three times as likely to have had a household member visit the FSM than were Hawaii households. Half of all migrant households in Guam had a household member return to the FSM compared to only 17 percent of the households in Hawaii, a difference that is statistically significant. This reflects the closer proximity of Guam than Hawaii to the FSM. It may also reflect the age of the migration flow to Hawaii. The high proportion of newly established households in Hawaii would have had less time to save for and to make a return trip home than the higher proportion of older, more established households in Guam.

"Social" expenditures

To date, no study has analyzed the influence that the participation by household members in ethnic-based social organizations and events has on remittance behavior. Participation in activities sponsored by the wider migrant community should have a positive influence on household remittance behavior because it encourages regular interpersonal contact among migrants from the same origin country (*see*, for example, Massey et al. 1987:145-147). Migrants who actively participate in these organizations and events will likely have a high proportion of personal network ties with other co-ethnics and a strong orientation to their culture and society of origin. This should discourage reneging and encourage the fulfillment of obligations, such as the need to care for aging parents, and should have a positive influence on both the probability of remitting and the amount remitted.

In this research, I include a single continuous variable that measures the amount of money spent on social events in the twelve months prior to the survey, as a percent of total annual household income. This social expenditures variable includes the amount of money spent by the household on weddings, funerals, religious celebrations, family "get togethers," and church donations. Because of the importance of these social events in Pacific Island cultures, they can be large and costly affairs and can be a significant drain on a household's budget. While the variable does represent an expenditure it is also a proxy for the household's level of integration into the wider Micronesian community. It is likely that the more a household spends on local social activities, the greater its integration into the local migrant network. This increased integration should positively influence household remittance behavior. Thus, as the level of household social expenditure increases the probability of remitting and the amount remitted should also increase.

Guam migrant households spend on average a higher proportion of their annual income on social expenditures than Hawaii households do. Table 7-1 shows that Guam households spend an average of 10 percent compared to the 6 percent spent by Hawaii households, a difference that is statically significant. This may again reflect the comparative age of the migration flows. The older, more established households in Guam may be able to spend a higher percentage of their income on social expenditures than the newly established households in Hawaii can. Also, the migrant community in Guam has a longer establishment history, which may mean there are simply more ethnic organizations and events in Guam than Hawaii, which would result in a higher social expenditure.

Receipt of remittances from overseas

The term "remittances" is usually used in the migration literature to refer to the resources sent by migrants to their family and friends in their countries of origin. However, remittances are bi-directional. Migrants send resources to non-migrants in their countries of origin, but they also receive money and goods from their families and friends abroad. If sending remittances overseas indicates active participation by migrant households in migrant networks, as I have argued, then the reverse is also true. Migrant households whose members receive remittances from overseas are also active participants in migrant networks. In this research, I include a dummy variable that indicates whether or not anyone in the household has received cash remittances from overseas in the past twelve months. The receipt of remittances from overseas, because it indicates the maintenance of a relationship between a migrant and non-migrant household, may be positively associated with both the probability of remitting and the amount remitted. However, migrant households that receive remittances may be experiencing financial instability and may be least able to remit. Thus, the receipt of remittances from overseas may be negatively associated with household remittance behavior.

As can be seen in table 7-1, only about 2 percent of all households in Guam received remittances from overseas. Because of the small number of cases, any results derived from the inclusion of this variable in the Guam analysis will have to be interpreted with caution. A higher percentage of households in Hawaii, about 13 percent, received remittances. These differences are statistically significant.

Language spoken at home

I include a dummy variable measuring the amount of English spoken at home as an indicator of the households' level of integration into the wider Guam and Hawaii societies. Newly established households whose members have poor English skills may be forced to rely heavily on the resources and assistance available through the migrant network. Research by Gurak and Kritz (1987: cited in Gurak and Caces 1992) among Dominican and Colombian migrants in New York City demonstrated an association between a reliance on migrant networks and poor English skills. They found that migrants who received a high number of different forms of assistance from relatives upon arrival were also those with poor English skills. The continued reliance by migrants on the ties established with kin and other co-ethnics could retard their ability to improve their English skills. This would perpetuate their dependence on the migrant network through time and slow their assimilation into the wider society. Conversely, newly established migrant households whose members have good English skills may be less dependent on contacts established through the migrant network. Less dependence on the migrant network would mean a more rapid adaptation and complete assimilation through time. Thus, I predict a negative association between the level of English spoken in the home and household remittance behavior.

The differences in the proportion that speak English at home in the Guam and Hawaii households are striking. As can be seen in table 7-1, over two-thirds of all households in Guam report not speaking English or another language more frequently than English compared to about half of all households in Hawaii. About one-quarter of the households in Hawaii speak only English, compared to 17 percent of the households in Guam. These differences are statistically significant.

Proportion of non-Micronesians in household

As a measure of household social endogamy, I include the proportion of non-Micronesians present in the household. A high proportion of non-Micronesians would effectively limit the number of origin society contacts that a migrant could gain by living with other Micronesian migrants. By increasing the number of society of destination contacts, migrants who live in households with a high proportion of non-Micronesians are likely to develop a high proportion of their immediate social ties outside the migrant network. By reducing their reliance on the migrant network, migrants reduce their level of interaction with other co-ethnics. This could shift their cultural orientation from the origin to the destination society. Thus, a high proportion of non-Micronesians in the household should be negatively associated with both the probability of remitting and the amount remitted.

It is not common for migrant households in either Guam or Hawaii to include non-Micronesians. Hawaii households are more likely to include non-Micronesians, which may reflect the higher proportion of non-family households. Approximately 6 percent of all households in Guam include non-Micronesians, compared to 16 percent in Hawaii. This difference is statistically significant.

"Social" Time

In this chapter, my measure of remittance duration is "social" time, including the years overseas of the earliest migrant and its square and the years since the arrival of the last migrant. These measures were discussed in some detail in chapter six (see pp. 132-136). None of the measures of migrant network participation included in the model are highly correlated with either "social" time variables. I predict that, once the network participation variables are controlled for statistically, the association between time and remittance behavior will remain positive. If so, this would suggest that network participation has no influence on the association between remittance behavior and time.

Household Financial Resources

The key measure of the influence of financial resources on remittance behavior is adult equivalent income. This measure was discussed in some detail in chapter five (see pp. 115-116). Both the adult equivalent income and its square are included in the model. As suggested by the results presented in both chapters five and six, a household's financial resources will be positively associated with both the probability of remitting and the amount remitted.

RESULTS

Network Participation and the Probability of Remitting

Table 7-2 shows the results of the logistic regression analyses on the likelihood (log odds) of remitting for both Guam and Hawaii migrant households, controlling for social time, household resources, and network participation. In both the Guam and Hawaii analyses, the percent of household income spent on social expenditures is positively associated while the level of English spoken in the home is negatively associated with the probability of remitting. The direction and significance of these coefficients supports the view that local network participation can increase remittance behavior while integration into the wider receiving society has a dampening effect. In the Guam analysis, a return trip home to the FSM by a household member has a strong, positive effect of the household's likelihood of remitting. The FSM trip coefficient is also positive in Hawaii but not statistically significant.

In the Guam and Hawaii "social" time analyses presented in chapter six (see table 6-2), both years overseas of the earliest migrant and its square are statistically significant, indicating the likelihood of remitting rises then declines as the years between the arrival of the first and last migrant increases. In the Guam analysis, the time since the arrival of the last migrant is also significant, indicating the probability of remitting declines as the years since last arrival increases. In the Guam and Hawaii analyses presented in this chapter, the "social" time variables maintain the same pattern of significance. All three "social" time variables in Guam and both years overseas of the earliest migrant variables in Hawaii remain significant. This suggests controlling for the influence of network participation has little influence over remittance duration in either Guam or Hawaii.

Adult equivalent income remains a strong positive predictor of the likelihood of remitting in Guam and Hawaii households. Both the linear and quadratic terms in both equations remain statistically

Table 7-2:   Multivariate Analysis of Network Participation on the
Likelihood (Log Odds) of Remitting with Controls for Other
Explanatory Variables, Guam and Hawaii, 1997

Explanatory Variable	Likelihood of Remitting (logistic regression)	
	Guam N=1,077	Hawaii N=784
Intercept	-2.050***	-1.561***
Remittance Duration		
Years Overseas of the Earliest Migrant	0.114**	0.183***
Years Overseas of the Earliest Migrant, Squared	-0.004*	-0.008***
Time Since the Arrival of the Earliest Migrant	-0.066**	-0.027
Household Resources		
Adult Equivalent Income	0.127***	0.102***
Adult Equivalent Income, Squared	-0.243***	-0.078***
Network Participation		
Social Expenditures as a Percent of Total Household Income	0.438**	3.073***
Percent of Non-Micronesians in Household	-1.418	-0.028
Trips to the FSM	1.268***	0.102
Receipt of Remittances by Household from Overseas	0.461	-0.157
English Use in the Home:		
Other and English Equally or Other Less Frequently than English	-0.433	-0.136
English Exclusively	-1.295***	-1.430***
Log Likelihood	1167.4	858.1

Note: Adult equivalent income and square are per $1,000. The non-transformed values of the linear and squared coefficients are as follows: for the Guam logistic equation, .000127 and –2.43E-9; and for the Hawaii logistic equation, .000102 and –7.75E-12.
(a) Reference category: other exclusively or other more frequently than English.
*Significant at p<.10. **Significant at p<.05. ***Significant at p<.01.

significant even after controlling for all other variables. These results underscore the fundamental importance of household resources in remittance decision-making.

Network Participation and the Amount Remitted

As with the logistic regression results, the results of the OLS analysis provide support for the positive influence of network participation on the amount remitted. Table 7-3 shows the results of the OLS regression analysis on the log of the amount remitted for both Guam and Hawaii migrant households, controlling for social time, household resources, and network participation. The results of the OLS analyses are very similar to the logistic results presented in the previous section. In both Guam and Hawaii, the level of English spoken in the household is negatively associated with the amount remitted, while the percent of social expenditures is positively associated only with the remittance behavior of Guam households.[xxx] Social expenditure is a strong indicator of the amount remitted in Guam. Each 10 percent increase in social expenditures is associated with a 2.7 percent increase in the amount of money remitted. Unlike the logistic results, the number of trips to the FSM is not significant in the Guam OLS analysis. It is significant in the Hawaii OLS analysis, but at a very high probability level (p=0.0919). These results suggest that local network participation and the level of integration into the wider society has a greater impact on the amount remitted than international network participation.

In Guam, both of the years overseas of the earliest migrant variables are significant, as they were in the "social" time baseline analysis presented in chapter six. In the Hawaii model, none of the remittance duration variables are significant, which is also consistent with the "social" time baseline analysis. This suggests that controlling for network participation has little influence on the association between time and household remittance behavior. Both adult equivalent income variables are also significant, as they were in the previous baseline models. A change in the adult equivalent income has a stronger influence on the amount remitted by the Guam households than by the Hawaii households. In Guam, each 10 percent increase in adult equivalent income is associated with a 0.87 percent increase in the amount remitted. In Hawaii, each 10 percent increase is associated with a 0.31 percent increase in the amount remitted.

Table 7-3:   **Multivariate Analysis of Network Participation on the Amount Remitted (Logged) with Controls for Other Explanatory Variables, Guam and Hawaii, 1997**

Explanatory Variable	Amount Remitted (OLS regression)	
	Guam N=403	Hawaii N=302
Intercept	4.690***	5.760***
Remittance Duration		
Years Overseas, Earliest Migrant	0.097**	-0.020
Years Overseas, Earliest Migrant, Squared	-0.004**	0.002
Years Since Arrival of Last Migrant	-0.025	-0.015
Household Resources		
Adult Equivalent Income	0.089***	0.031**
Adult Equivalent Income, Squared	-0.136***	-0.024*
Network Participation		
Social Expenditures as a Percent of Total Household Income	0.280***	0.027
Percent of Non-Micronesians in Household	0.186	-0.235
Trips to the FSM	-0.020	0.300*
Receipt of Remittances by Household from Overseas	0.719***	0.330
English Use in the Home:		
Other and English Equally or Other Less Frequently than English	-0.269	-0.402**
English Exclusively	-0.477**	-0.499**
R-squared	0.170	0.084

Note: Adult equivalent income and square are per $1,000. The non-transformed values of the linear and squared coefficients are as follows: for the Guam OLS equation, .000089442 and $-1.358133E-9$; for the Hawaii OLS equation, .000031183 and $-2.41629E-10$.
(a) Reference category: other exclusively or other more frequently than English.
*Significant at p<.10.   **Significant at p<.05.   ***Significant at p<.01.

CONCLUSION

Network theory suggests the participation by household members in migrant networks helps maintain remittance levels through time. Network participation results in increased levels of remittance behavior because it retards the migrants' adaptation to and assimilation into the host society. By encouraging migrants to maintain a high level of social ties with other co-ethnics and an orientation to the culture and society of origin, network participation also encourages migrants to maintain their relationships with non-migrants overseas and continue remitting. By maintaining the relationships in which remittances are exchanged, network participation should have a positive influence on both the probability of remitting and the amount remitted.

The results presented in this chapter do provide support for a positive association between network participation and household remittance behavior. While there are some differences in the results of the Guam and Hawaii analyses, the statistical significance of two variables support the hypothetical link between the level of migrant integration and household remittance behavior. The first variable, the level of English use in the home, was consistently significant throughout all four models. The second variable, the percent of total household income spent on social expenditures, was significant in three of the four models. Both of these variables are proxies measuring, in different ways, a household's degree of integration into the migrant network and the wider receiving society. I argued that higher levels of English use in the home should be positively associated with integration into the wider receiving society and negatively associated with remittance behavior. The results of both the Guam and Hawaii logistic and OLS regression analyses support this association. Households that only speak English are both less likely to remit and remit less than those households that speak another language exclusively or another language more frequently than English. Because it reflects the amount of money households spend on culturally significant activities, social expenditures measures the household's level of integration into the wider migrant community. Thus, higher levels of social expenditure should be positively associated both with integration into the migrant community and remittance behavior. Again, the results of the Guam logistic and OLS analyses and the result of the Hawaii logistic analyses support this association. Households that spend a higher percentage of their total income on social expenditures are more likely to remit and remit at higher levels than are households that spend less on social expenditures. These results support my argument that migrant network participation influences remittance behavior by first influencing the rate of adaptation and assimilation migrants experience in the host society.

"Local" and "International" Aspects of Network Maintenance

What is also interesting about the results of the analyses is that both of these variables, the level of English use in the home and the percent of total household income spent on social expenditures, reflect local migrant network activity. The measures of network participation included in the analyses can generally be divided into "local" and "international" aspects of migrant network maintenance. The local aspects refer to those activities that occur among the migrants settled overseas and in their country of destination, including, as I mentioned above, language use and social expenditures. The international aspects refer to those activities that occur between migrants and non-migrants, such as the exchange of remittances and visits home. It is interesting that, for the most part, the local aspects of network maintenance were significant while the international aspects were not. While not conclusive, this suggests that the continued participation by migrants in local network activity is more important for remittance behavior than participation in international network activity.

That being said, the most significant difference between the Guam and Hawaii logistic regression results was the significant, positive influence of return trips to the FSM on Guam households' likelihood of remitting. Return trips home is classified as an international aspect of network maintenance. However, because of the proximity of Guam to the FSM and the relative low cost of airfare between the islands, the significance of the variable in the Guam analysis may be reflecting the regional basis of the migrant network. Circular migration between Guam and the FSM is so common that migrants are seen as "virtually commuters" (1994 Census of Population and Housing: National Report 1996:153). By comparison, return migration from Hawaii to the FSM is not as easy or as cheap. Visits to the FSM from Hawaii are considered international, not regional, travel, with ticket costs reflecting this difference. This helps explain why the proportion of Hawaii households with a member who visited the FSM in the past year is so low and why the return trip variable is insignificant in the Hawaii analyses.

Network Participation and Time

The results presented in this chapter support my hypothesis (hypothesis 3, see chapter 2, p. 41). Households whose members participate in migrant networks are more likely to remit and remit at higher levels than are those households whose members isolate themselves from migrant networks. But does network participation help maintain migrant household remittances *through time*? The results of the analyses provide no direct evidence of this. Migrant network participation, especially local participation, reinforces remittance behavior. However, controlling for the influence of network participation appears to have little influence on the relationship between time and remittance behavior.

CHAPTER 8
Conclusion

The results presented in chapters five through seven suggest several general conclusions about the relationship between time and remittance behavior. First, as predicted by the remittance decay hypothesis, remittance behavior declines through time. When time is measured at the household level, three of the four baseline models presented in chapter five (table 5-5) indicate a significant quadratic relationship between remittance behavior and the passage of time. These results indicate that both the probability of remitting and the amount remitted rise, peak, and decline through time.

Second, the change in the probability of remitting and the amount remitted through time reflects the migration process, specifically family reunification migration. To incorporate the influence of the household reconstitution process on remittance behavior, the time overseas of the earliest migrant (or "household time") was divided into two periods of "social time" to account for the influence of the migration process on household reconstitution. These include 1) the period of additional migration, the time between the arrival of the earliest and latest migrants, and 2) the period of no additional migration, the time after the arrival of the last migrant. The results of the expanded baseline analyses (table 6-2) show that the longer it has been since the household has received a migrant member, the less likely that household is to remit. This suggests that households that have completed the family reunification process are less likely to remit, while households in the process of reconstituting overseas are more likely to remit. Combined with the results of qualitative research on Pacific Island migrant communities, the results suggest remittance decay reflects the process of household reconstitution overseas, specifically family reunification migration. Remittances begin as a migrant household "extension" is established overseas, continue as the household receives new members, and end with the arrival of the last dependent from the country of origin. Thus, family reunification appears to be the underlying social process that drives remittance duration and decay.

Third, while the migration process, especially the process of family reunification, explains why remittances decline through time, it also helps explain why in some migrant communities remittances continue over long periods. Households with dependent members in the country of origin will continue remitting until all of those members have either joined the migrant household overseas or until their dependence on the migrant household has ended. The results of the Guam logistic regression analyses presented in chapter six (table 6-3) provide support for this view of household remittance duration. Guam households with a history of continued and family reunification migration are more likely to remit than are those households that have never received additional migrant members. Both continued and family reunification migration have a greater influence on the probability of remitting than on the amount remitted, which is influenced more by a household's financial resources.

Fourth, time works indirectly on household remittance behavior, especially the probability of remitting, through the process of continued migration. A number of the variables included in the regression analyses, including the number of migrant "waves" and the family reunification dummy variable, measure events that occur within the period of continued migration and reflect the passage of time. This helps explain why, when they are included in the analyses, the remittance duration variables are no longer significant (see chapter six, tables 6-3 and 6-4). Because time indirectly influences remittance behavior through the process of continued migration, time is more significant for those households reconstituting overseas through family reunification than for those households who members migrated at the same time. That is, households establishing themselves through family reunification migration will continue remitting as long as it takes to complete the reconstitution process. Households established through family migration, where all the immediate kin ties migrate at once, will not remit because the reconstitution process is completed at the point of arrival in the country of destination.

Finally, network participation, by slowing the rate of adaptation and assimilation to the receiving society, can have a positive influence on household remittance behavior, including both the probability of remitting and the amount remitted. The results of the analyses presented in chapter seven (tables 7-2 and 7-3) suggest that "local" network participation, or interaction with other migrants in the country of destination, has a greater influence on household remittance behavior than "international" network participation, or interaction with non-migrants in the country of origin. While network participation can positively "boost" both the probability of remitting and the amount remitted, it apparently has little to no influence on the association between time and household remittance behavior.

THE SOCIOLOGICAL APPROACH TO REMITTANCE BEHAVIOR

A sociological approach to remittance behavior, as I have outlined it in this research, focuses on the relationships that exist between migrants and non-migrants. These relationships are of paramount importance because they form the social basis of remittance behavior. Their continued existence helps explain what remittances are, why migrants remit, and why remittance behavior continues through time. Remittances are the resources exchanged between the migrant and non-migrant members of migrant social networks. They occur as the result of migrants' participation in those networks and represent the their efforts to build and maintain social capital. Remittances are not simply "sent" by migrants to non-migrants. Rather, they are exchanged for resources accessible through the maintenance of relationships with other network members. Migrants will continue to remit as long as the relationships in which remittances are exchanged are maintained. By focusing on the relationships between migrants and non-migrants, the sociological approach also helps to explain *why* remittances decline through time. Remittance behavior declines and eventually ends largely because the relationships between migrants and non-migrants have substantially altered or have ceased to exist. For example, the economic independence of dependent non-migrants in the country of origin would alter the migrant/non-migrant relationship and would end the need for remittances from migrants overseas. Also, the migration of non-migrants to join migrants overseas would end the remittance relationship and remittance behavior. The death of non-migrants would also end this relationship.

By explaining why remittances continue through time *as well as* why they end, the sociological approach helps explain remittance behavior in general and not just a single aspect, such as remittance decay. However, because of the importance of remittances to many labor-exporting countries, it is understandable why researchers and policy makers have been most concerned with remittance decay, especially determining those factors that positively influence aggregate remittance levels through time. This concern with aggregate remittance levels has had two unfortunate side effects for remittance research. First, it has encouraged researchers to focus on remittances as a resource (i.e., simply as money or goods) rather than the product of the migrant/non-migrant relationship. By focusing on the outcome of remittance behavior, research has placed greater emphasis on determining those factors that influence the remittance event (i.e., the exchange of remittances) rather than the social context in which the event occurs. In other words, they are trying to determine factors that influence the "effect" without first considering the "cause" of the outcome.

Second, the emphasis on explaining aggregate remittance levels has placed little pressure on researchers to clarify the causes of remittance behavior. Stark's (1978; Lucas and Stark 1985; Stark and Lucas 1988) view of altruism, the concern migrants have for the well being of their non-migrant family members, seems to be generally accepted by researchers as the root cause of remittance behavior. Stark's work is almost universally cited and few alternatives to the theory of altruism and remittance decay have been proposed.[xxxi] According to Stark, as the altruism migrants have for their kin back home weakens both the incidence and amount of remittances will decline through time. However, Stark never clarifies why this is so. Because of the importance of aggregate remittances to many labor-exporting economies, this lack of theoretical development is understandable. The theoretical cause of remittance behavior is far less important than ascertaining those immediate determinants which, if positively manipulated, could help maintain high remittance levels through time.

By placing emphasis on remittances as a resource and failing to clarify the causal process, it is not surprising that the research literature has generated conflicting results regarding the association between time and remittance behavior (see chapter two). By comparison, the sociological approach focuses on the migrant/non-migrant relationship in which remittances are exchanged. It is the existence of these relationships that helps explain why remittances exist, why they continue through time, and why they end. In this sense, the sociological approach "backs up the causal chain" and incorporates the cause (i.e., the migrant/non-migrant relationship), the event (i.e., the exchange of remittances), and the effect (i.e., the amount and frequency) of remittance behavior into a single framework. The incorporation of a plausible causal process into a theory of remittance behavior that can explain both remittance duration and decay is one of the more significant contributions of this research.

IMPLICATIONS FOR FUTURE RESEARCH

The results of this research have implications for future studies of remittance behavior, especially those focusing on the remittance levels through time. Two of these addressed methodological issues and were discussed in depth in earlier chapters. These include: 1) modeling remittance behavior and duration at the household level and 2) recognizing that certain variables, such as household size or income, can act as indirect measures of time and reduce the significance of the remittance duration variables in the regression analyses. Also, as discussed in chapter four, the age and composition of the migration flow can determine community characteristics, such as the proportion of single migrants or the average age of migrant households, that can help explain remittance behavior. Establishment histories are especially important when attempting to explain the differences in the remittance behavior of two migrant communities, as was clearly demonstrated in this research.

The results suggest two additional, more substantive issues that are also important when comparing the remittance behavior of different migrant groups. Both of these issues are significant because they influence the rate of the migration process. The first is the distance of the migrant community from the country of origin. Migrants living in communities far from their home countries may find it difficult to return to visit. This could have two effects on household reconstitution and, indirectly, remittance behavior. The cost associated with return trips home may encourage migrants to move with their families overseas. This would significantly reduce or eliminate the active period of remittance behavior and minimize aggregate remittance levels. Conversely, the costs associated with migrating may force households reestablishing themselves overseas to reconstitute more slowly, thus extending the period of chain migration. This would significantly increase the active period of remittance behavior and would positively influence aggregate remittance levels. Close proximity to the country origin could have two effects on household reconstitution and remittance behavior as well. If return trips home arc easy and affordable, migrants may be encouraged to act as "commuters" or "transnational migrants" (Portes et al. 1999), maintaining two households in the origin and destination areas. This could prolong the separation of dependent family members and encourage continued remitting (*see* Basch, Schiller, and Szanton-Blanc 1994; Goldring 1998; Mahler 1998; Schiller, Basch, and Blanc-Szanton 1992).

Conversely, migrating may be easier and more affordable, which may mean that migrants are encouraged to move with their family members. Also, cheaper migration costs may shorten the period of chain migration needed to establish a household overseas. Both of these would reduce or eliminate the period of active remittance behavior and would negatively influence aggregate remittance levels.

A second important issue when comparing the remittance behavior of migrant communities is the disparities in the standard of living in both the origin and destination areas. The standard of living can influence the resources (both financial and informational) available to the migrant household to initiate and complete the migration process. In the country of origin, the standard of living may determine if the members of a household move overseas at once or if they need to establish a household "extension" and chain migrate through time. The standard of living in both the countries of origin and destination can effect the rate migrant households complete the migration process by either increasing or decreasing their ability to chain migrate and reestablish themselves overseas. This would influence the period of active remittance behavior and aggregate remittance levels through time.

Thus, both the proximity of the migrant community to the country of origin and the standards of living in both the sending and receiving areas can influence the rate of the migration process. By altering the period of time it takes for the average migrant household to reconstitute overseas, these characteristics can either extend or reduce the period of active remittance behavior. This can, in turn, either positively or negatively influence aggregate remittances levels. Differences in these characteristics can help explain the variable patterns of remittance behavior found among different migrant communities.

GENDER AND REMITTANCE BEHAVIOR

One additional advantage of adopting the sociological approach to analyze remittance behavior is that it allows the researcher to explain things that were not addressed by other theories. For example, virtually without exception, women tend to be more frequent remitters than men are even though they lack the same earning capacity (Connell and Brown 1995; Curran 1995, 1996; DeJong, Richter, and Isarabhakdi 1995). While women may not send the same level of remittances as men do, they have been found to remit a higher proportion of their net incomes (Vete 1995). This behavior can be explained when the gendered nature of networks, social ties, and social capital is considered. Research has clearly demonstrated that social networks are gendered, that is, there are distinct differences between the networks of women and men (Greenwell, Burciaga Valdez and DaVanzo 1997; Matthei 1996). A greater proportion of women's social ties are to kin, and they rely on kin for support more than men. This reliance on kin makes women more active members in their social networks, using their social capital to exchange resources and information. This exchange makes them more aware of what is going on and what is needed back home. It has been argued that women have a much better understanding of household needs throughout the Pacific (Stanwix and Connell 1995), which may be partly attributable to their traditional responsibility for household maintenance (Connell and Brown 1995).

However, this awareness of household needs may also reflect their need to maintain the ties with family network members in the country of origin that provide social capital. Female migrants are often in a more precarious economic position in their countries of destinations than male migrants. They are less likely to be employed, and when they are employed, they frequently work in sex-segregated occupations that offer low wages and few benefits (Boyd 1989; Pedraza 1991). Female migrants may have a greater need and therefore be motivated to make more of an effort to maintain those ties in case they need financial or emotional help in the future. The higher remittance rate of women reflects this effort to maintain social capital.

The research literature has not adequately addressed the influence of gender on remittance behavior. Because of the traditional emphasis on explaining individual remittance behavior, remittance research has simply included gender as an individual-level characteristic. While gender is certainly an individual-level characteristic, its influence on remittance behavior is best explained within the context of households. One interesting area of research would be to divide migrant households by family type (e.g., married couple, female-headed, and male-headed households) and analyze the influence of the gender of the household head on remittance behavior. A final future research agenda, then, is to determine if female-headed households are more active remitters than either married couple or male-headed households.

Notes

[i] While Stark and Lucas (1988) assume that altruism will wane through time, they never explicitly state why. This is a common problem in many of Stark's writings on remittance behavior. Terms such as "a change in the intensity and nature of kinship relations," "change in commitments," "change in the perception of rural needs," and "change in the attachment to rural areas" pepper his work, which seems to suggest an unfortunate tautology: altruism, the concern migrants have for the well-being of their families back home, wanes through time because time reduces the concern migrants have for their families' well-being.

[ii] In a study of remittances in Kenya, Knowles and Anker (1981) found that approximately 90 percent of all remittance transfers in their sample were between parents, children, spouses, and siblings. Only approximately 11 percent were between in-laws and friends and other relatives.

[iii] The Compact of Free Association between the United States and the FSM and RMI went into effect in late 1986 and with Palau in late 1994. These three countries together make up what is frequently called the Freely Associated States. The Compact, as a joint congressional-executive agreement, charts the relationship between the United States and the three island nations. Under the Compact, the United States funds the FSM, RMI, and Palau for a range of development programs and provides them with the use of United States currency, immigration privileges, federal processing of applications for air services, United States transportation of mail, and other benefits. In exchange, each Pacific nation guarantees the United States exclusive use of its land for military purposes. The Compact of Free Association is discussed in greater detail in Chapter 4.

[iv] Households were defined as FSM, Palauan, or Marshallese based on the ethnicity of the householder. This means that for every household defined, for example, as FSM, there is at least one household member (but probably more) who is from the FSM.

ᵛ This section is based on information from an internal report, *The Status of Micronesian Migrants in 1998: A Study of the Impact of the Compacts of Free Association Based on the Censuses of Micronesian Migrants in Hawaii, Guam and the Commonwealth of Northern Mariana Islands,* written by the International Program Committee, Bureau of the Census for the Office of Insular Affairs, Department of the Interior and through personal conversations I had with the staff of the International Programs Center.

ᵛⁱ These variables included household income, state and island of origin of the household head, family type, total count of the household, monthly electricity bill, monthly water bill, monthly rent, annual expenditure on weddings and funerals, the amount of remittances sent overseas, the total amount of remittances received by all individuals in the household, the number of children less than 6, between 6 and 17, and less than 18 in the household, and the household zip code.

ᵛⁱⁱ Removing the households of the children of Micronesian migrants reduced the Guam sample size by 11 from 1,081 to 1,070 and the Hawaii sample size by 48 from 828 to 780.

ᵛⁱⁱⁱ Using the earliest migrant from the FSM rather than the householder actually increased the Guam sample from 1,070 to 1,078 and the Hawaii sample from 780 to 791. This is because the eight households on Guam and three households in Hawaii that were defined as non-FSM households based on the ethnicity of the householder became classified as FSM households when based on the ethnicity of the earliest migrant.

ⁱˣ The natural logarithm of the amount remitted by remitting households is used as the dependent variable in the OLS analyses. The mean logarithm of this variable is 5.66 for Guam and 5.92 for Hawaii migrant households.

ˣ Technically speaking, Spain claimed both the Caroline islands, which consists of both the FSM and the Republic of Palau, and the Marianas, which consists of both Guam and the Commonwealth of the Northern Marianas.

ˣⁱ The TTPI included the present-day island nations of the FSM, the Republic of Palau, the Republic of the Marshall Islands, and the Commonwealth of the Northern Marianas.

ˣⁱⁱ Unlike most territories and commonwealths of the United States, the CNMI has maintained control over its immigration policy. As of 1989, there were 15,000 alien laborers in the CNMI (Hezel and McGrath 1989:57).

xiii Depending on the FSM state, Guam is between 500 and 1,400 miles from the FSM. Honolulu is between 2,800 and 4,300 miles, while Los Angeles is between 5,400 and 6,600 miles from the FSM.

xiv This is the estimate of the population without the duplicate households discussed earlier in Chapter 3. The original count was 3,024, including duplicate households.

xv According to the US Census Bureau, there were 5,846 people living in Hawaii in 2000 who reported "Micronesia" as their place of birth. This number would include migrants from the FSM as well as other Micronesian countries, such as Palau, the Marshall Islands, and Kiribati (Census 2000, Summary File 3).

xvi According to the US Census Bureau, there were 16,469 people living in the United States in 2000 who reported "Micronesia" as their place of birth. This number would include migrants from the FSM as well as other Micronesian countries, such as Palau, the Marshall Islands, and Kiribati (Census 2000, Summary File 3).

xvii This pattern in the Hawaii data persisted even after dividing the total sample into family v. non-family households, number of years overseas by earliest migrant (less than five and more than five, and less than ten and more than ten), percent of adults in the labor force (quartiles), whether or not the earliest migrant migrated for school, and whether or not the earliest migrant worked in the agricultural industry or in an agricultural occupation.

xviii I use logistic regression to analyze the probability of remitting. However, I recognize that the logits (or log odds) produced are not probabilities but likelihoods. In this research, I use the terms *probability of remitting* and *likelihood of remitting* interchangeably.

xix In the Micronesian Census, the householder was usually the person, or one of the persons, in whose name the house was owned or rented and who was listed as person one on the Census questionnaire. If no such person existed, the respondents or the enumerator selected any household member age 15 years or older as the householder.

xx This is true for both Guam and Hawaii. For Guam, the earliest migrant has been overseas for an average of 7.63, compared to an average of 6.78 years for the migrant householder. In Hawaii, the earliest migrant has been overseas an average of 6.22, compared to an average of 5.27 for the migrant householder. The difference in the mean between the earliest migrant and the migrant householder in both Guam and Hawaii was found to be statistically significant using a two-tailed t-test and a p-value of less than 0.001.

[xxi] In Hawaii, the earliest migrant has been overseas on average for 6.24 years, compared to an average of 3.17 for all other migrant household members. This is a difference of 3.07 years. In Guam, the earliest migrant has been overseas for 7.67 years, compared to an average of 4.17 years for all other migrant household members. This is a difference of 3.50 years (see table 4-1).

[xxii] In this research, adult equivalent income and its square have been adjusted to a per $1,000 scale. The linear term was divided by 1,000. This term was then squared and divided by 100.

[xxiii] The quadratic equation $a+bt+ct^2$, where a=intercept, b=the linear coefficient, c=the squared coefficient, and t=time, has a first derivative maximum of c<0 at the value of t=-b/2c. The maximum is derived as follows: $0=a+bt+ct^2$; 0=b+2ct; -b=2ct; t=-b/2c. For Guam, t=-(.119/((2)(-.005))) = 11.9 years. For Hawaii, t = 9.69 years.

[xxiv] The correlation between the number of adult and the proportion of working migrants in the household in Guam and Hawaii is very low. In Guam, the correlation is 0.02; in Hawaii, it is –0.03.

[xxv] The nuclear family included the presence or absence of either 1) the spouse and child(ren) or 2) the spouse and/or children. There were not statistical differences in the models. The family of orientation included the nuclear family (with spouse and/or children) and households with the earliest migrant's parent(s) and/or sibling(s). The extended family included the nuclear family (with spouse and/or children), the family of orientation, and households with any other relative of the earliest migrant.

[xxvi] If the spouse of the earliest migrant was not present in the household, the second time period (i.e., the time between the arrival of the spouse and earliest migrant) was equal to zero. If there was only one migrant in the household, then the first two time periods were equal to zero.

[xxvii] The logistic regression chi-square values increase as "blocks" of variables are included in the analysis. The chi-square of the baseline model (consisting of the time and income variables only) is 98.75 for Guam and 109.50 for Hawaii. When the number and proportion of adult migrants are included in the analysis, the chi-square increases to 122.38 for Guam and 163.13 for Hawaii. When the continued migration and family reunification variables are included, the chi-square increases to 136.68 for Guam and 165.60 for Hawaii. All of these chi-square values are significant at p<0.0001.

[xxviii] The R-squared values increase as "blocks" of variables are included in the analysis. The R-squared of the baseline model is .116 for Guam and .032 for Hawaii. When the number and proportion of adult migrants are included in the analysis, the R-squared values increase to .139 for Guam and .040 for Hawaii. When the continued migration and family reunification variables are included, the R-squared variables increase to .143 for Guam and .055 for Hawaii.

[xxix] This is true for both the Hawaii and Guam migrant communities. In Hawaii, single migrant households have an average household income of $12,600 compared with $23,000 for households established through family reunification migration and $13,500 for households established through family migration. The comparative numbers for Guam are $10,600, $19,600 and $13,800.

[xxx] In the Guam analysis, whether or not the household received remittances was also found to positively influence the amount remitted. Although the receipt of remittances was found to significantly influence the amount remitted, it was included in the analysis as a control variable to maintain comparability with the Hawaii analysis. The positive influence on the amount remitted is in the expected hypothetical direction, but because so few Guam households received remittances, its statistical significance is questionable.

[xxxi] One exception is Poirine's (1997) "implicit family loan arrangement." In many ways, this framework represents an extension of Stark's work, which Poirine acknowledges (p. 590).

References

Ahlburg, Dennis A. 2000. "Poverty Among Pacific Islanders in the United States: Incidence, Change, and Correlates." *Pacific Studies* 23:51-74.

Ahlburg, Dennis A. and Richard P.C. Brown. 1998. "Migrants' Intentions to Return Home and Capital Transfers: A Study of Tongans and Samoans in Australia." *Journal of Development Studies* 35:125-145.

Appleyard, Reginald T. and Charles W. Stahl. 1995. *South Pacific Migration: New Zealand Experience and Implications for Australia.* International Development Issues, 42, Australian Agency for International Development. Canberra: CPN Publications.

Ballendorf, Dirk A. 1977. "Education in Micronesia: Is There a Brain Drain Coming?" *Micronesian Perspective, A Contemporary Review* 1:4-8.

Banerjee, Biswajit. 1984. "The Probability, Size, and Uses of Remittances from Urban to Rural Areas in India." *Journal of Development Economics* 16:293-311.

Barringer, Herbert, Robert W. Gardner, and Michael J. Levin. 1993. *Asians and Pacific Islanders in the United States.* New York: Russell Sage Foundation.

Basch, Linda, Nina Glick Schiller, and Cristina Szanton Blanc. 1994. *Nations Unbound: Transnational Projects, Postcolonial Predicaments, and Deterritorialized Nation-States.* Basel, Switzerland: Gordon and Breach Publishers.

191

Bordieu, Pierre. 1986. "The Forms of Social Capital." Pp. 241-258 in *Handbook of Theory and Research for the Sociology of Education*, edited by J.G. Richardson. New York: Greenwood.

Boyd, Monica. 1989. "Family and Personal Networks in International Migration: Recent Developments and New Agendas." *International Migration Review* 23:638-670.

Breen, Richard. 1996. *Regression Models: Censored, Sample-Selected or Truncated Data*. Series/Number 07-111. Thousand Oaks, California: Sage Publications.

Brown, Richard P.C. 1997. "Estimating Remittance Functions for Pacific Island Migrants." *World Development* 25:613-626.

----------. 1998. "Do Migrants' Remittances Decline over Time? Evidence from Tongans and Western Samoans in Australia." *The Contemporary Pacific* 10:107-151.

Burkhauser, Richard V. and Timothy M. Smeeding. 1996. "Relative Inequality and Poverty in Germany and the United States Using Alternative Equivalence Scales." *Review of Income and Wealth* 42:381-400.

Burt, Ronald S. 1992. *Structural Holes*. Cambridge: Harvard.

Coleman, James. 1988. "Social Capital in the Creation of Human Capital." *American Journal of Sociology* 94:S95-S120.

Connell, John. 1980. *Remittances and Rural Development: Migration, Dependency, and Inequality in the South Pacific*. Occasional Paper No. 22, National Centre for Development Studies. Canberra: Australian National University.

Connell, John and Richard P.C. Brown. 1995. "Migration and Remittances in the South Pacific: Towards New Perspectives." *Asian and Pacific Migration Journal* 4:1-33.

Curran, Sara R. 1995. "Gender Roles and Migration: 'Good Sons' vs. Daughters in Rural Thailand." *Seattle Population Research Center Working Paper No. 95-11*. University of Washington.

----------. 1996. "Intrahousehold Exchange Relations: Explanations for Education and Migration Outcomes." *Seattle Population Research Center Working Paper No. 96-5*. University of Washington.

Curson, P.H. 1979. "Migration, Remittances and Social Networks among Cook Islanders." *Pacific Viewpoint* 20:185-198.

Curtis, Richard. 1986. "Family and Inequality Theory." *American Sociological Review* 51:168-183.

DeJong, Gordon, Kerry Richter, and Pimonpan Isarabhakdi. 1995 "Gender, Values, and Intentions to Move in Rural Thailand." *International Migration Review* 30:748-770.

Durand, Jorge, William Kandel, Emilio A. Parrado and Douglas S. Massey. 1996. "International Migration and Development in Mexican Communities." *Demography* 33:249-264.

Ellis, Mark, Dennis Conway and Adrian J. Bailey. 1996. "The Circular Migration of Puerto Rican Women: Towards a Gendered Explanation." *International Migration* 34:31-64.

Faeamani, Sione 'U. 1995. "The Impact of Remittances on Rural Development in Tongan Villages." *Asian and Pacific Migration Journal* 4:139-155.

Folbre, Nancy. 1986. 1986. "Cleaning House: New Perspectives on Households and Development." *Journal of Development Economics* 22:5-40.

Forsyth, David J. 1992. *Migration and Remittances in the South Pacific: Forum Island Countries*. Monograph. Suva: University of the South Pacific.

Franco, Robert. 1985. *Samoan Perceptions of Work: Moving Up and Moving Around*. New York: AMS Press.

(FSM) Federated States of Micronesia National Census Office. 1996. *1994 FSM National Census of Population and Housing: National Census Report.* Pohnpei, FSM: Office of Planning and Statistics.

Funkhouser, Edward. 1992. "Migration from Nicaragua: Some Recent Evidence." *World Development* 20:1,209-1,218.

----------. 1995. "Remittances from International Migration: A Comparison of El Salvador and Nicaragua." *The Review of Economics and Statistics* 77:137-146.

Glick Schiller, Nina, Linda Basch, and Cristina Blanc-Szanton. 1992. "Transnationalism: A New Analytical Framework for Understanding Migration." Pp. 1-24 in *Towards a Transnational Perspective on Migration: Race, Class, Ethnicity, and Nationalism Reconsidered.* New York: Annals of the New York Academy of Sciences 654.

Goldring, Luin. 1998. "The Power of Status in Transnational Social Fields." Pp. 165-195 in *Transnationalism from Below*, edited by M.P. Smith and L.E. Guarnizo. New Brunswick: Transaction Publishers.

Gorenflo, Larry, J. 1993. "Demographic Change in Kosrae State, Federated States of Micronesia." *Pacific Studies* 16:67-118.

----------. 1995. "Regional Demographic Change in Chuuk State, Federated States of Micronesia." *Pacific Studies* 18:47-118.

Gorenflo, Larry J. and Michael J. Levin. 1991. "Regional Demographic Change in Yap State, Federated States of Micronesia." *Pacific Studies* 14:97-145.

----------. 1992. "Regional Demographic Change in Pohnpei State, Federated States of Micronesia." *Pacific Studies* 15:1-49.

----------. 1995. "Changing Migration Patterns in the Federated States of Micronesia." *ISLA: A Journal of Micronesian Studies* 3:29-71.

Gos, Jon and Bruce Lindquist. 1995. "Conceptualizing International Labor Migration: A Structuration Perspective." *International Migration Review* 29:317-351.

Granovetter, Mark S. 1973. "The Strength of Weak Ties." *American Journal of Sociology* 78:1,360-1,380.

Grasmuck, Sherri and Patricia R. Pessar. 1991. *Between Two Islands: Dominican International Migration.* Berkeley: University of California Press.

Greenwell, L., R. Burciaga Valdez and Julie DaVanzo. 1997. "Social Ties, Wages, and Gender in a Study of Salvadorean and Pilipino Immigrants in Los Angeles." *Social Science Quarterly* 78:559-577.

Grieco, Elizabeth M. 1998. "The Effects of Migration on the Establishment of Networks: Caste Disintegration and Reformation Among the Indians of Fiji." *International Migration Review* 32:704-736.

----------. 2001. *The Native Hawaiian and Other Pacific Islander Population: 2000.* US Census Bureau Census 2000 Brief C2KBR/01-14. US Government Printing Office: Washington, DC.

Grieco, Elizabeth M. and M. Boyd. 1998. "Women and Migration: Incorporating Gender Into International Migration Theory." Center for the Study of Population, Florida State University, Working Paper 98-139.

Gurak, Douglas T. and Fe Caces. 1992. "Migration Networks and the Shaping of Migration Systems." Pp. 150-176 in *International Migration Systems: A Global Approach,* edited by M.M. Kritz, L.L. Lim and H. Zlotnik. New York: Oxford University Press.

Gurak, Douglas T. and Kritz, M.N. 1987. "Los Patrones de Migracion de los Dominicanos y de los Colombianos en la Ciudad de New York: El Rol de las Redes de Parentesco." Pp. 153-184 in *La Inmigracion Dominicana en los Estados Unidos,* edited by J. del Castillo and C. Mitchell. Universidad APEC: Santo Domingo.

Hartmann, Heidi. 1981. "The Family as a Locus of Gender, Class and Political Struggle: The Example of Housework." *Signs* 6:366-394.

Heckman, John. 1979. "Sample Selection Bias as a Specification Error." *Econometrica* 47:153-161.

Hezel, Francis N. 1978. "The Education Explosion in Truk." *Micronesian Reporter* 26:24-33.

Hezel, Francis N. and Michael J. Levin. 1990. "Micronesian Emigration: Beyond the Brain Drain." Pp. 42-60 in *Migration and Development in the South Pacific*, edited by J. Connell. Pacific Research Monograph 24. Canberra: National Centre for Development Studies.

----------. 1996. "New Trends in Micronesian Migration: FSM Migrants to Guam and the Marianas, 1990-1993." *Pacific Studies* 19:91-114.

Hezel, Francis N. and Thomas B. McGrath. 1989. "The Great Flight Northward: FSM Migration to Guam and the Northern Mariana Islands." *Pacific Studies* 13:47-64.

Ho, Christine G.T. 1993. "The Internationalization of Kinship and the Feminization of Caribbean Migration: The Case of Afro-Trinidadian Immigrants in Los Angeles." *Human Organization* 52:32-40.

Hoddinott, John. 1992. "Modelling Remittance Flows in Kenya." *Journal of African Economies* 1:206-232.

Hondagneu-Sotelo, Pierrette. 1992. "Overcoming Patriarchal Constraints: The Reconstruction of Gender Relations Among Mexican Immigrant Men and Women." *Gender and Society* 6:393-415.

Hondagneu-Sotelo, Pierrette. 1994. *Gendered Transitions: Mexican Experiences of Immigration*. Berkeley: University of California Press.

James, K.E. 1997. "Reading the Leaves: The Role of Tongan Women's Traditional Wealth and Other 'Contraflows' in the Processes of Modern Migration and Remittance." *Pacific Studies* 20:1-27

James, K.E. 1993. "The Rhetoric and Reality of Change and Development in Small Pacific Communities." *Pacific Viewpoint* 34:135-152.

James, K.E. 1991. "Migration and Remittances: A Tongan Village Perspective." *Pacific Viewpoint* 32:1-23.

Johnson, G.E. and W.E. Whitelaw. 1974. "Urban-Rural Income Transfers in Kenya: An Estimated-Remittances Function." *Economic Development and Cultural Change* 22:473-479.

Katz, Eliakim and Oded Stark. 1986. "On Fertility, Migration and Remittances in LDCs." *World Development* 14:133-135.

Knowles, James C. and Richard Anker. 1981. "An Analysis of Income Transfers in a Developing Country." *Journal of Development Economics* 8:205-226.

Lin, Nan. 2001. "Building a Network Theory of Social Capital." Pp. 3-29 in *Social Capital: Theory and Research*, edited by N. Lin, K. Cook, and R.S. Burt. New York: Aldine De Gruyter.

Lomnitz, L. 1976. "Migration and Networks in Latin America." Pp. 133-150 in *Current Perspectives in Latin American Urban Research*, edited by A. Portes and H.L. Browning. Austin: University of Texas Press.

Loomis, Terry. 1990. "Cook Island Remittances." Pp. 61-81 in *Migration and Development in the South Pacific*, edited by J. Connell. Pacific Research Monograph 24. Canberra: National Centre for Development Studies.

Lucas, Robert E.B. and Oded Stark. 1985. "Motivations to Remit: Evidence from Botswana." *Journal of Political Economy* 93:901-918.

Macpherson, Cluny. 1985. "Public and Private Views of Home: Will Western Samoan Migrants Return?" *Pacific Viewpoint* 26:242-262.

----------. 1994. "Changing Patterns of Commitment to Island Homelands: A Case Study of Western Samoa." *Pacific Studies* 17:83-116.

Mahler, Sarah J. 1998. "Theoretical and Empirical Contributions Toward a Research Agenda for Transnationalism." Pp. 64-100 in *Transnationalism from Below*, edited by M.P. Smith and L.E. Guarnizo. New Brunswick: Transaction Publishers.

Massey, Douglas S. and Lawrence C. Basem. 1992. "Determinants of Savings, Remittances and Spending Patterns among US Migrants in Four Mexican Communities." *Sociological Inquiry* 62:185-207.

Massey, Douglas S., Rafael Alarcon, Jorge Durand and Humberto Gonzalez. 1987. *Return to Aztlan: The Social Process of International Migration from Western Mexico*. Berkeley: University of California Press.

Massey, Douglas S., Joaquin Arango, Graeme Hugo, Ali Kouaouci, Adela Pellegrino, and J. Edward Taylor. 1993. "Theories of International Migration: A Review and Appraisal." *Population and Development Review* 19:431-466.

Mattheai, Linda M. 1996. "Gender and International Labor Migration: A Network Approach." *Social Justice* 23:38-53.

Menjivar, Cecilia, Julie DaVanzo, Lisa Greenwell and R. Burciaga Valdez. 1998. "Remittance Behavior Among Salavadoran and Filipino Immigrants in Los Angeles." *International Migration Review* 32:97-126.

Munro, Doug. 1990. "Transnational Corporations of Kin and the MIRAB System: The Case of Tuvalu." *Pacific Viewpoint* 31:63-66.

Myles, John. 1996. "Social Transfers, Changing Family Structure and Low Income Among Children." *Canadian Public Policy* 22:244-267.

Oberia, A.S. and H.K. Manmohan Singh. 1980. "Migration, Remittances and Rural Development: Findings of a Case Study in the Indian Punjab." *International Labour Review* 119:229-241.

Pedraza, Sylvia. 1991. "Women and Migration: The Social Consequences of Gender." *Annual Review of Sociology* 17:303-325.

Peoples, James G. 1986. "Employment and Household Economy in a Micronesian Village." *Pacific Studies* 9:103-120.

Pessar, Patricia R. 1999. "Engendering Migration Studies: The Case of New Immigrants in the United States." *American Behavioral Scientist* 42:577-600.

Poirine, Bernard. 1997. "A Theory of Remittances as an Implicit Family Loan Arrangement." *World Development* 25:589-611.

Portes, Alejandro. 1995. "Economic Sociology and the Sociology of Immigration: A Conceptual Overview." Pp. 248-279 in *The Economic Sociology of Immigration: Essays on Networks, Ethnicity and Entrepreneurship*, edited by A. Portes. New York: Russell Sage Foundation.

----------. 1998. "Social Capital: Its Origins and Applications in Modern Sociology." *Annual Review of Sociology* 24:1-24.

Portes, Alejandro and Julia Sensenbrenner. 1993. "Embeddedness and Immigration: Notes on the Social Determinants of Economic Action." *American Journal of Sociology* 98:1,320-1,350.

Portes, Alejandro, Luis E. Guarnizo, and Patricia Landolt. 1999. "The Study of Transnationalism: Pitfalls and Promise of an Emergent Research Field." *Ethnic and Racial Studies* 22:217-237.

Raj, S. 1991. *Fiji-Indian Migration to Sydney*. Masters of Arts thesis, Department of Geography, University of Sydney.

Ravallion, Martin and Lorraine Dearden. 1988. "Social Security in a 'Moral Economy': An Empirical Analysis for Java." *Review of Economics and Statistics* 70:36-44.

Rempel, Henry and Richard A. Lobdell. 1978. "The Role of Urban-to-Rural Remittances in Rural Development." *Journal of Development Studies* 14:324-341.

Rosenzwieg, Mark R. and Oded Stark. 1989. "Consumption Smoothing, Migration, and Marriage: Evidence from Rural India." *Journal of Political Economy* 97:905-926.

Rubinstein, Donald H. and Michael J. Levin. 1992. "Micronesian Migration to Guam: Social and Economic Characteristics." *Asian and Pacific Migration Journal* 1:350-385.

Russell, Sharon Stanton. 1986. "Remittances from International Migration: A Review in Perspective." *World Development* 14:677-696.

Schmertmann, Carl P. 1995. "An Introduction to Nonparametric Regression in Demographic Research." *European Journal of Population* 11:169-192.

Shankman, Paul. 1976. *Migration and Underdevelopment: The Case of Western Samoa*. Boulder: Westview Press.

Small, Cathy A. 1997. *Voyages: From Tongan Villages to American Suburbs*. Ithaca: Cornell University Press.

Stanwix, Clare and John Connell. 1995. "To the Islands: The Remittances of Fijians in Sydney." *Asian and Pacific Migration Journal* 4:69-87.

Stark, Oded. 1978. *Economic-Demographic Interaction in the Course of Agricultural Development: The Case of Rural-to-Urban Migration*. Research Report No. 2/78. Tel Aviv: David Horowitz Institute for Research of Developing Countries.

----------. 1980. "On the Role of Urban-to-Rural Remittances in Rural Development." *Journal of Development Studies* 16:369-374.

----------. 1985. *Altruism and Beyond: An Economic Analysis of Transfers and Exchanges within Families and Groups.* Cambridge: Cambridge University Press.

Stark, Oded and David E. Bloom. 1985. "The New Economics of Labor Migration." *American Economic Review* 75:173-178.

Stark, Oded and David Levhari. 1982. "On Migration and Risk in LDCs." *Economic Development and Cultural Change* 13:191-196.

Stark, Oded and Robert E.B. Lucas. 1988. "Migration, Remittances, and the Family." *Economic Development and Cultural Change* 36:465-481.

Stark, Oded and J. Edward Taylor. 1989. "Relative Deprivation and International Migration." *Demography* 26:1-14.

Stark, Oded, J. Edward Taylor and Shlomo Yitzhaki. 1986. "Remittances and Inequality." *The Economic Journal* 96:722-740

Tilly, C. and Brown, C.H. 1967. "On Uprooting, Kinship, and the Auspices of Migration." *Journal of Comparative Sociology* 8:141-164

Tongamoa, Taiamoni. 1987. *Migration, Remittances and Development: A Tongan Perspective.* Master of Arts thesis, University of Sydney.

US Department of the Interior, Office of Insular Affairs. 1997. *Census of Micronesian Migrants to Hawaii and Guam.* Unpublished data.

US Department of the Interior, Office of Insular Affairs. 1998. *Census of Micronesian Migrants to the Commonwealth of Northern Marianas.* Unpublished data.

Vete, Mele F. 1995. "The Determinants of Remittances among Tongans in Auckland." *Asian and Pacific Migration Journal* 4:55-68.

Wellman, Barry and Scot Wortley. (1990) "Different Strokes from Different Folks: Community Ties and Social Support." *American Journal of Sociology* 96:558-88.

Wolfson, Michael and John M. Evans. (1990) *Statistics Canada's Low-Income Cut-Offs: Methodological Concerns and Possibilities.* Analytical Studies Branch: Statistics Canada, Ottawa.

Index